Ethics in Higher Education

ETHICS IN
HIGHER
EDUCATION

Case Studies for Regents

By Alexander B. Holmes

Preface by Hans Brisch

Foreword by Harold L. Enarson

Sponsored by the Regents Education Program,

Oklahoma State Regents for Higher Education

UNIVERSITY OF OKLAHOMA PRESS : NORMAN AND LONDON

Bear in mind in reading *Ethics in Higher Education: Case Studies for Regents* that any resemblance to actual events, locales, or persons, living or dead, is entirely coincidental.

Library of Congress Cataloging-in-Publication Data

Holmes, Alexander B. (Alexander Bradley), 1947–
    Ethics in higher education : case studies for regents / by Alexander B. Holmes; preface by Hans Brisch; foreword by Harold L. Enarson.
        p.   cm.
    ISBN 0-8061-2857-7 (alk. paper)
    1. Universities and colleges—Administration—Moral and ethical aspects—Case studies. 2. Universities and colleges—United States—Administration—Case studies. 3. College administrators—Professional ethics—United States—Case studies. I. Title.
    LB2341.H586   1996
    378.1'01—dc20   95-47001
                                                               CIP

Text design by Debora Hackworth

The paper in this book meets the guidelines for permanence and durability of the Committee on Production Guidelines for Book Longevity of the Council on Library Resources, Inc.∞

1   2   3   4   5   6   7   8   9   10

Contents

Preface

Under a new state law establishing the Regents Education Program, Oklahoma's 155 regents and trustees must take fifteen hours of continuing education related to their duties as higher education board members. Two of the fifteen hours must be in ethics. The ethics requirement is a sign of the times in Oklahoma and in the nation. Actions of public officials are under close scrutiny, and well they should be. Regents and trustees, although generally unknown to the public, hold the fate of the institution, its students, and even society in their hands. Regents and trustees lead by example and action, and their ethical standards must be of the highest caliber.

This book of ethics case studies for regents and trustees was developed because of a void in the literature and because of the need for ethics materials in the Oklahoma Regents Education Program. The case studies and variants are designed around six key areas of university governance and attempt to enlighten sincere, well-meaning board members as to the ethical dilemmas facing them at every turn.

HANS BRISCH
Chancellor
Oklahoma State Regents for Higher Education

Foreword

Justice John Paul Stevens of the U.S. Supreme Court once commented that, although it may be impossible to define pornography, "We know it when we see it." It would be tempting—but wrong—to apply the same definition to ethical behavior. To be sure, the most obvious transgressions of law and ethics are easily recognizable: bribes, kickbacks in contracts, favoritism in employment, misappropriation of funds, falsification of official records, and theft. But there is a large domain of human behavior that, although beyond the reach of the law, is unethical.

It was wrong (and stupid) for Stanford University to charge upkeep of the Stanford Mausoleum to "research overhead," for a distinguished medical researcher at the University of Pittsburgh to look the other way in the face of fraud, for the University of California leadership to provide superplush golden parachutes for themselves. It is always wrong, that is to say, unethical, for a purchasing officer to accept a kickback or for a coach to woo a blue chip athlete with cash. Wrong, and also stupid, since the likelihood of getting caught red-handed is substantial. Unfortunately, self-deceit makes for feelings of invincibility—witness the professor who gave fresh meaning to "full time" by teaching on a full-time basis at three campuses in different cities.

The men and women who serve on governing boards of colleges and universities operate largely in the shadows of public attention. It is rare that a regent or trustee comes under fire in the press. This is not to say that there are not on occasion gross ethical violations on the part of governing board members. As in governing bodies everywhere, there are always a few unscrupulous board members, indifferent to ethical norms, who are hell-bent on pursuing an individual agenda. I think of trustees who act as grand inquisitors investigating whatever bothers them on the campus, who micromanage the department or college of their choice, and who *order* the president to hire the candidate of their choice for the number two job in the university.

More often than not a violation of law and ethics that becomes a media target involves a regent messing with the sports program. (History affords no reported instance of a governing board member making improper overtures in recruiting an oboe player for the band.) I am reminded of trustees who *demand* a fistful of tickets to games and who ride roughshod over established procedures in hiring coaches. As a longtime student of governing boards, I have concluded that almost nothing can be done about these bad actors except, in rare instances, discipline imposed by their colleagues.

Happily, the great majority of trustees care deeply about their institutions, and they work long and hard at one of the most challenging and important volunteer jobs in the nation. Good trustees easily identify and avoid blatant violations of ethical norms. However, well-meaning members of governing boards can easily stumble into ethical violations, unaware of the harmful consequences on the integrity of the institution. Indeed, they do it all the time, as any experienced president will attest. Ethical issues come up in the normal course of events—in a phone call, a letter, an agenda item. The red flag of danger may show, but often there is only the palest yellow light of caution.

Trustees acquire instant "old friends" when they assume office—friends who want a job or want the president fired or want an architectural contract or (very commonly) want preference in admissions to a professional school. Some requests for help are easily dismissed, but others raise serious questions about the propriety of the request. Is the board member being induced to be unethical?

As Alexander Holmes notes in his Introduction to this book, regents have power, and this is the source of potential ethical problems. It is so very easy for individual board members to engage in actions that, on reflection, are clearly unethical. How to minimize their doing so is a matter that has haunted the Association of Governing Boards and writers on governance. It does little good to exhort trustees to be good guardians of the integrity and welfare of their institutions. But it may do some good to help trustees understand in great depth and with more sophistication what is required of good—yes, ethical—trustees. In such instruction, the case method has no peer, as the schools of law, business, and public administration have learned. It is in that tradition that this book was prepared.

The cases presented here are more than entertaining stories (fiction extracted from experience). They are invitations to think more deeply and get to the heart of the matter in issues that are, or should be, controversial. As such, these studies will serve as a ready-made instructional tool for conscientious governing board members trying to understand the complexities of their responsibilities. Governing board members who work through these carefully constructed cases will be rewarded for their efforts with a new sensitivity to the possibility that significant ethical issues lurk everywhere.

Finally, these cases lay bare, often indirectly, the values that must undergird good trusteeship. At bottom, ethics deal with values at work, and the case studies here sharply pose such questions as, What values do trustees stand for and why? This small book invites introspection on the part of governing board members. As such, it fills a conspicuous gap in the literature. It is also a useful reminder that governing boards are, for better or worse, role models for the university community. Will they behave in exemplary fashion, or will they contribute to the flood tide of cynicism about the American dream?

HAROLD L. ENARSON
President Emeritus
The Ohio State University

Introduction

This book is intended to provide thought-provoking discussion of the ethical issues faced by regents and trustees of institutions of higher education. The focus is on publicly supported colleges and universities, although many of the same issues are faced by those charged with setting policy at private institutions of higher education.

This book's thinness belies the importance of the material covered. No greater harm can come to an institution than for it to become embroiled in controversy by a breach of ethical conduct, actual or perceived, whether by a regent or by an employee of the institution. This case study book is neither a "how-to" handbook nor a prescription for ethical behavior. Indeed, anyone who thinks such an item exists should resign her or his position of public trust immediately. Ethical behavior is like morals: it cannot be legislated. But this fact has not stopped attempts at legislative prescriptions.

Let me state, here at the beginning, that I am not an attorney. All legislative attempts to proscribe and prescribe the behavior of regents and other public officials are subject to interpretation, and without benefit of formal training, I have placed my own interpretations on many of these matters. In some sense, this is exactly what regents must do as they face the many ethical dilemmas that come with their appointments.

Certain behavior, however, is strictly out of bounds. But simply staying within the letter of the law will not guarantee that a tone of ethical conduct is established, and it is the *tone* of acceptable ethical behavior set by the board that will permeate the entire institution to either the benefit or the detriment of the students and public who are to be served. A case can be won in a court of law but lost in the court of public confidence.

We may be tempted to say that it is sad that there is a need for such a book as this. However, several recent headline-grabbing cases of ethical failures by regents and college/university administrators and staff clearly document such a need. This, I think, is the result of closer scrutiny by the press and public of all of society's institutions. We are living in an age of greater accountability, and the standards of acceptable conduct are being more closely examined. The role of business leaders has gone through an intense period of scrutiny, often because of legal and financial problems that have come to light. Savings and loan scandals, insider trading on Wall Street, and the behavior of corporate presidents and board members during take-over bids are but a few of the recent examples.

We are also living in an age in which the public has shown a distrust of and disgust with governmental institutions at all levels. A required vote of the people on all tax increases and limitations on elected officials' terms of office are both statements of the public's lack of confidence in government. Since the mid-1980s an unprecedented number of elected officials, from county commissioners to sitting U.S. senators, have been indicted and found guilty or left office in disgrace. The primary reason for their demise has been some breach of ethics, not felonious acts.

Institutions of public higher education play an important role in modern American society. It is little wonder, then, that in an age of general skepticism colleges and universities are becoming more and more the focus of scrutiny. This means that the behavior of regents who are charged with setting policy at these institutions will be subjected to ever-closer review, as will the behavior of the faculty and staff.

I hope that this book will find an audience among those persons with the capability to encourage the public's confidence in our institutions of higher education, because no institution in society can be a positive force for progress without the confidence of the public. Colleges and universities in the United States have served the public well by contributing to general economic growth through the advancement of knowledge, and by providing an avenue for individuals' achievement on the basis of ability alone. Without our colleges and universities, social mobility in the United States would be almost nonexistent. But institutions of higher education will perish if they cannot pass the public's close scrutiny because of the inability of regents, faculty, and staff to adhere to the highest standards of ethical behavior. It is in the belief that this unique institution in our society can be preserved and strengthened for future generations that this book has been written, and to this goal it is dedicated.

Acknowledgments

I owe a debt of gratitude to many, both for the opportunity to write this book and the experiences that allow me to write with any sense of realism. Chancellor Hans Brisch, Ruth Ann Dreyer, and Ned Bastow, of the Oklahoma State Regents for Higher Education, had the vision for such a volume and the confidence that I could provide it. Their encouragement and efforts to enhance the state of ethics among the many members of higher education governing boards in Oklahoma are gratefully acknowledged, as are the editing efforts of Carolyn Maxwell of the State Regents' staff for polishing and toning the text.

Through the Regents Education Program I have had the opportunity to interact with Oklahoma college and university regents and trustees. The efforts of these dedicated public servants as they wrestled with the ethical conundrums I presented gave me both real-world experience with the issues and confidence that institutions of higher education can and are ethically overseen by lay boards of citizen appointees.

I have been fortunate to serve on many boards of state agencies, both as member and as chair. These experiences have provided me with fodder for much of what follows and a firsthand understanding of a board member's role and the relationship one member must have with another to reach a common goal. I thank my colleagues on these boards and the executive directors and staffs of these agencies for the educational experiences they provided—and for their patience as I learned my lessons.

Finally, I thank Oklahoma Governor Henry Bellmon for the confidence he showed in me as his appointed Secretary of Finance and Revenue and State Budget Director. Without this experience, this book would have simply been an academic's view of the world. My debt of gratitude to Governor Bellmon extends well beyond this appointment, however. He leads by example with the highest standards of ethics, providing a "sense of the right thing" in public service. It is from him that I learned that ethical behavior in public service is not an effort; it is simply what we should expect from ourselves if we are to serve faithfully with honor.

ALEXANDER B. HOLMES

Ethics in Higher Education

Chapter 1

Regents and trustees attain their governing board positions in different ways in different states. Some "win" the position by election to office in a constituent group. Elected examples include the president of the student body or the alumni association and a statewide elected official, such as the superintendent of education. Most regents, however, receive their authority through the political appointment process, which requires that the governor make an appointment and the state senate confirm it. By this method, the position of regent becomes part of the political patronage system.

This recognition of political patronage is not meant to degrade the regents' positions but to point out the obvious: regents are part of the democratic process and serve only because they caught the favor of the governor and survived the confirmation process. Regents typically serve terms with durations extending beyond that of their appointing authority, the rationale for which is to provide independence and autonomy for institutions of higher education.

Historical precedents abound in which institutions of higher education had their very existence threatened by shifting political winds. At an earlier time, the appointment of university presidents was among the first patronage positions filled by incoming governors. Now, the structure of a lay governing board is a compromise, subject indirectly to the proper pressures of the democratic process but insulated from the overt control of a particular administration. Although change can be made in response to the demands brought by the political process, it must be effected through sustained pressure rather than edicts of a volatile or ephemeral nature.

An understanding and appreciation for the source of a regent's power are important for putting the issues of ethical behavior in perspective. Although the position of regent may be one of political patronage, it is not a part of the executive branch of government in the same sense as, for example, an administrative post in the office of the governor is. The position of regent transcends a particular administration. The oath typically taken by regents on confirmation is to the people of the state, not to a particular party or administration. This accountability can, and will, cause conflicts between regents and the very authority by which they gained their position of power.

And regents do have power. The myriad decisions they make in a typical board meeting affect many individuals and businesses profoundly. Faculty members' academic careers, students' future educational opportunities, and businesses' revenues are all subjects of discussion and decisions at board meetings. Even though regents create policy through a vote, thus diminishing an individual regent's influence, the individual power vested in each regent cannot be ignored.

It is this power that is the source of potential ethical conflicts, making it necessary to carefully review all governing-board decisions in the context of their ethical considerations. A sobering exercise in unraveling thorny ethical issues is for regents to simply remind themselves of the considerable power they wield and ask for whose benefit they are to use this power. In the words of Thomas Jefferson, "Commerce between master and slave is despotism."

The Role of a Regent

In reading the case studies that follow, regents may find it helpful to ask what their role is or should be. More broadly, regents need an understanding of the governing board's place in the structure of a governmental agency to determine the "solutions" to the cases presented. In addition, regents must ask themselves what type of regent they wish to become and what role they wish to play in the governance of the institution.

All persons who accept an appointment to a board of regents of a state college/university are assumed to have the best intentions for the institution and the state. Service on a board takes significant time away from other activities and also subjects regents to the sometimes harsh glare of public scrutiny. The position of regent instantly makes a person a public official, and in a legal sense the regent becomes a "public figure" for many circumstances. Simply put, a regent's private life will be reviewed, and he or she will have an almost impossible hurdle to overcome in any action of libel or slander.

The question of the type of regent a person wishes to be is not answered simply by saying, "A thoughtful, judicious, and ethical regent." Nor should the answer include the area of the university in which the regent might wish to become specialized. By an almost natural process, some regents will take a special interest in financial affairs or affirmative hiring practices or contract research activities or some other area. Colleges and universities are such large and diverse institutions that specialized expertise on the part of regents is a positive and beneficial allocation of time, although becoming an "expert" in a particular area in no way relieves a regent of accountability for fulfilling all the duties assigned the particular board by law. A regent cannot delegate this accountability either de facto or de jure.

Just how involved should a regent become in the day-to-day affairs and management of the college/university? Should a regent attempt to mediate personnel disputes among midlevel managers? Should a regent become involved in the admissions process on a case-by-case basis? Just how deep into the administrative structure of the institution should a regent reach without reviewing the issue with the president? Conversely, should a regent interact only with the president and senior administrative officials as they report at the monthly or quarterly meetings?

All regents will be approached at one time or another with requests to intercede in all sorts of matters. There may be an assertion that the administration is acting too slowly in responding to an inquiry, a faculty member has been derelict in her or his responsibilities, or space was filled in the desired dormitory before a friend's daughter or son applied. A regent must balance the need and responsibility to be informed on the institution's quality of management with the ethical concerns that surround inquiries on behalf of particular individuals. Regents have power, and regardless of how a regent makes an inquiry, the person responding will feel that power. The further down into the administrative structure a regent goes with a request to "please follow up for me," the greater the differential in power becomes.

However, regents who never question reports from the president will soon find they know very little about the institution they are charged with governing. In the private sector members of corporate boards of directors have been made personally liable for illegal actions of the company on the grounds that they were charged with the oversight of all aspects of corporate policy. This situation has led to a good deal more probing by board members. The body of law governing personal liability of regents resulting from negligence in managing the affairs of their institution is sufficiently complex that no general statement can be made as to the limits of such liability. Suffice it to say that regents should be cognizant that they have a positive duty to be informed thoroughly on all matters affecting their school.

Presidents, of course, would rather be the sole source of information to regents, and they consider regents who make independent inquiries as meddlers. A balance must be reached, and only on careful reflection can regents decide where that balance lies. If that point is carefully chosen and not amended without good cause, regents will find natural and consistent solutions to the ethical issues they confront.

Generally stated, the role of a regent is to set policy and determine if it has been carried out properly. Management decisions are left to managers, and if they manage poorly, then they are to be replaced. The president is in some sense the sole employee of the board, and if the president's staff consistently mismanages, then it falls to the board to replace the president, not the offending employees. If regents wish to engage in hiring, individual employee review, promotion, and firing decisions, then they should apply for the job of president. If board members feel that they *must* make these types of decisions, then they should replace the president with someone in whom they have confidence.

There are special cases of direct employees of the board. In addition to the secretary of the board, who typically provides clerical and scheduling skills, some boards have found it beneficial to hire internal auditors and attorneys. Sometimes the ombudsperson, if such a position exists, reports directly to the board of regents. In the main, however, regents deal with the senior management staff exclusively and leave middle and lower-level managers, including academic department chairs, to make executive decisions that do not require prior approval of the board.

From the point of view of ethical considerations, the more a regent becomes involved with the day-to-day operations of the college or university, the more likely she or he is to breech some canon of ethical conduct. As the cases in this book are presented, the reader may want to consider just how involved in the daily management of the institution a regent should or might become and how this involvement will impact the ethical issues of each case. I hope that these cases will help as regents struggle with the critical issue of defining their role and then redefining it through experience.

Chapter 2

A Taxonomy of Ethical Issues

Ethical issues can be categorized in any number of ways. One simple method is to organize them according to the structure provided by statutory prohibitions: abuse of power, conflict of interest, violation of freedom of speech, and other prohibited acts. The real world of a regent, however, does not come in such neat packages. This book therefore presents ethics cases according to six areas of university governance:

1. Financial issues
2. Academic issues
3. Personnel issues
4. Student press
5. Student athletics
6. Campus organizations

Because regents make most of their policy decisions in these areas, they are the areas where most ethical considerations arise.

Financial Issues

Even relatively small colleges and universities are large financial enterprises with critical budget issues determining the priorities of the institution and the ability of the various units to provide services to students and the public. Tuition rates and student fees, the allocation of funds by college and department, and the level of salary increases (or decreases) are but a few of the difficult decisions that face regents. In addition, institutional budgets are developed in ways that seem, at first, confusing to most regents because private-sector budgeting, which may be familiar to some regents, bears little resemblance to its public-sector counterpart. Even the national accounting standards applicable to institutions of higher education are different from those of other public-sector entities.

Ethical concerns involving the budgeting process are almost exclusively related to the purchasing process. A tuition increase that may reduce the number of students who will be able to attend college is not viewed as an ethical issue, nor is the lack of a pay raise that will result in faculty leaving for other positions. These, and a thousand other similar, very difficult decisions, are in the nature of policy and do not test the personal ethics of a regent.

This is not to say that these policies do not have broad social implications that regents must weigh conscientiously. The distinction being drawn here is between personal ethics, which concern the person of the regent, and social ethics, which apply to the institution. For example, the implication of a tuition increase on minority students is a serious matter of social ethics, but it should not call into question the personal ethics of a regent who in good conscience votes for that tuition increase to provide needed funding for the school.

Apart from salary payments to administrators, faculty, and staff, colleges and universities purchase billions of dollars of goods and services every year. Many goods are purchased through standing contracts that are let once a year, allowing the purchasing process to proceed in a timely way for standard products such as paper, plumbing and electrical supplies, and so on. Other items, such as food and motor fuel, that change price frequently are bid more often to enable the school to take advantage of potential savings. Items purchased at infrequent intervals are usually related to a particular project, such as new construction or renovation of buildings, and include the services of contractors, architects, suppliers, and others. The procurement process for this last type of purchase usually involves regents directly.

Regents are nevertheless responsible for all contracts, whether individual bids are reviewed and discussed by the board or the board simply affirms the actions of staff. The procurement process is one that should be thoroughly understood by all regents, and clear policy on the size of a contract or purchase that can be made *without* regent approval should be well developed and understood by regents and staff.

A case will be presented that tests a regent's relationship with potential vendors, friends, other regents, and the staff of the institution. Certainly a conflict of interest would exist between a regent and the public's welfare if an institution were to have a regent as a vendor. No one can be both master and servant. The case presented and the variant on it will examine just how far this conflict may extend.

The purchasing process also gives rise to ethical issues in the area of openness in government. The public is a party to all actions by regents, but when should the public be allowed to know? What role should an individual regent play in providing information to a potential vendor, who is, after all, a member of the public? These will be some of the questions raised in the case study of financial issues.

Academic Issues

Since institutions of higher education are by their very nature academic, regents must make policy decisions concerning the academic issues that fulfill the mission of the college/university. These issues deal with a diverse set of policy questions. What should be the admission standards to the various colleges? What should be the retention and graduation standards? What constitutes academic misconduct? How should academic misconduct by a faculty member or a student be handled? What are the due process considerations of any actions by the board?

All colleges and universities should have detailed catalogs and/or handbooks that clearly state the official policy of the board so that answers to most questions can be found quickly and easily. Regents, administrators, faculty, staff, and students rely on the guidelines set forth in these publications, although there are always exceptions to the rules. A student can appeal for an exception solely on the basis of extenuating circumstances. This avenue of appeal is based on the premise that the institution should provide a humane environment by allowing opportunities for individual judgment to determine the outcome of unique cases. Sometimes these exceptions must be ratified by the board of regents.

Cases of academic misconduct by a faculty member or a student are of a much more serious nature because they involve dishonesty in some form. Examples include plagiarism by a student of a class assignment, plagiarism of an academic paper by a faculty member, and cheating on an examination. The college/university handbook should provide a very detailed description of the procedures by which an accusation of academic misconduct is appropriately handled, as well as the penalties that can be imposed. These can range from letters of reprimand to dismissal from the university for both faculty and students. Because the potential penalties can be so severe, the procedure is usually structured to provide access to counsel and various due process guarantees in the criminal justice system. An aggrieved party will always have access to the courts if he or she does not receive satisfaction through the administrative process.

Regents should be aware that at some time they will most likely become judges in the academic appeal process because a regents' hearing is usually the final phase of the appeal process. This is certainly the case when a faculty member is involved and the recommended penalty is dismissal. In these cases, the board of regents sits as a court *en banc.* Just as the judicial system should not be corrupted by prejudice and ex parte communications (pleading the case to the judge privately out of court), the appeal process of academic misconduct must be free of prejudice and bias. This requires that regents conduct themselves as a court judge should and abide by the ethical standards of judges.

The case will deal with the role of a regent as judge in matters that affect a faculty member's relationship to her classroom performance and academic freedom. Personnel actions that may end in termination and the destruction of a faculty member's reputation will be presented. Variations on the case will focus on the issue of academic freedom and the relationship of the faculty member to a member of the board of regents.

Personnel Issues

From a management perspective, personnel issues are often the thorniest in both the public and the private sectors. This reflects the vital role employees play in the delivery of services, as well as the complex law surrounding any adverse action against an employee. Even small colleges and universities employ hundreds of workers, and large universities employ thousands, each of whom is guaranteed certain rights by both state and federal laws.

Every institution of higher education should provide a handbook to all employees describing their rights and general responsibilities. These handbooks will differ from those that deal with academic issues, although academic misconduct can lead to personnel action. Although these two areas are presented separately here to highlight the particular issues in each, both areas are clearly intertwined. Although staff employees cannot typically engage in academic misconduct, faculty can be guilty of breaches of personnel policy, such as sexual harassment.

The hiring procedures of a college/university can be separated into two very distinct parts: the procedures affecting faculty and those affecting staff. (Perhaps senior staff with academic appointments, such as deans, provosts, and the chief operating officer of the institution, constitute a third group, but the procedures for this group closely parallel the procedures affecting faculty hiring.) Staff hiring procedures are very similar to those in the private sector. Job posting requirements, job descriptions, the relationship between supervisor and employee, and the grievance process all closely align with private-sector employment practices. Faculty hiring (and related personnel actions such as pay raises, promotion, and the tenure process) is, however, very different. Faculty employees figure very prominently in the hiring, promotion, and compensation of their collegial faculty members/employees. This organizational structure is called a collegial model, meaning that employees are colleagues and that little distinction is made between supervisors and employees.

In the collegial model, faculty committees make recommendations on all personnel actions. These recommendations are reviewed by other committees of faculty members and eventually by deans, the president, and the board of regents. Depending on the particular college or university, the power of the faculty committees' recommendations can be taken very seriously, and administration changes from these recommendations are viewed as an attack on the collegial structure of the institution. Regent action that does not follow the faculty committees' recommendations is similarly suspect. Guidelines typically require written explanations for any variation to committee recommendations.

Although the collegial model has the drawback of potentially allowing self-perpetuation of substandard performance, it generally serves the university well. Controversial issues can be aired, and mutually agreeable accommodations can usually be reached. In addition, significant staff functions are handled by faculty committees, thereby reducing overhead expenses. (Interestingly, the so-called Japanese model of management currently in vogue is simply a variant of the collegial model that has been in place in American colleges and universities for decades.) Although the collegial model vests certain prerogatives in faculty committees, and all personnel actions must carry a recommendation of the president, the board of regents is the final authority and must bear the ultimate responsibility for personnel decisions. Failure to do so is an abrogation of regental responsibility.

From time to time, the board of regents, as the ultimate employer, must sit as judge in personnel disputes. As discussed earlier, a regent must be able to perform this function in an unbiased manner so that all possibilities of conflicts of interest are avoided. Statutory guidelines make it clear that a regent cannot be expected to act in an impartial manner if the issue involves an immediate relative. Consequently, antinepotism rules have been put in force. These vary in the definition of the degree of blood or affinity that is considered "too close."

A board of regents is a small groups of individuals who must work well together if they are to govern effectively. Even though one regent may withdraw from decisions that affect a relative, the other regents may feel an allegiance to the withdrawn member that could cloud their judgment in the matter before the "court." For this reason, an *unacceptable* solution to this situation is for the relative-regent to withdraw from all decisions involving a relative.

Regents must be aware that they, too, are susceptible to breaches of personnel guidelines affecting employees. Because regents have power over all employees at their institution, faculty, staff, and students are out of bounds for amorous relationships. Since sexual harassment, a serious offense, is deemed an abuse of power, this type of conduct is easily a serious breach of ethical behavior.

The case presented will deal with the potential conflict involved in nepotism. The issue of what constitutes an "employment action" by the regents and what ability a regent has to avoid a conflict by recusing (withdrawing) from the board action are addressed. A varient to the case explores these issues in the context of outside advisory boards.

Student Press

Newspapers written, managed, and edited by students for distribution to faculty, staff, other students, and the public are often a vital part of a college/university community. These newspapers, and news broadcast programs on some campuses, serve as laboratories and teach skills that are a basic part of journalism students' educational experience. Usually a committee of faculty and students chooses the students who will hold the paper's key management positions, and a faculty adviser serves as a sounding board for student reporters and editorial staff. As with any student laboratory experience, the product will show the signs of inexperience and growth.

These news publications are usually supported by advertising revenues, which are generated by a student sales force, and student fees. Even though most staff positions are nonsalaried, more often than not general educational funds from the college/university are required to meet expenses. Philosophically, student newspaper budgets are the same as the educational expenses associated with any academic program that requires laboratory equipment.

Legal precedent clearly states that student newspapers, whether fully or partially funded by general education dollars, must be viewed as "real" newspapers in virtually every respect. Furthermore, student newspaper "owner-ship" is not vested in the administration or the board of regents in matters of freedom of the press. Although administrators of colleges/universities are often frustrated that the student newspaper is not a "house organ" similar to private-sector newsletters from management, numerous cases have been decided in the federal courts forbidding prior restraint of news articles or *any* activity by school administrators that attempts to manage the news. Although school newspapers may be closed as part of a general reduction in services associated with budget cuts, the courts do not allow administrators to close student newspapers in an attempt to muzzle the press. Courts look to *intent* in these cases and have in the past ordered the newspapers reopened.

Regents who are placed in the difficult position of being charged with general oversight of all college/university activities find that this portion of their domain is protected from close management. Freedom of the press places the student publication not outside regent control but within regent control only when there is no intent to manage or censor the news. It is the duty of a free press to provide unbiased reporting of all relevant events, regardless of whether such reporting embarrasses the university.

Regents have a broader duty to provide the public with all information on the activities of the institution of higher education over which they exercise policy control.

21

To assure that the public has access to information concerning the school's activities, many states have enacted open-meeting and open-records laws. The press, both student and private sector, uses these laws to view most university records. Although some records are protected by specific state laws and some federal laws (the primary one being the so-called Buckley amendment, which protects students' records from nonconsensual disclosure), generally speaking all college and university records are subject to public view. In addition, all meetings of the regents must be publicly posted and must include an agenda that clearly states the actions that will be considered.

The public is always a party to any action of the regents of a public institution of higher education, and the press is the vehicle by which the public becomes informed of officials' actions. The student press, even though a laboratory for amateur reporters and editors, deserves no less respect as an agent for informing the public. Indeed, it is advisable for officials to spend extra time with student reporters to assure that they understand the issues of a story. The story will be written in any case, and it behooves a public official to be sure that those who will report the event are as knowledgeable of the facts as possible.

A persistent reporter on the trail of a story that will not show the school in its most positive light can be nettlesome, particularly when scarce university funds support the student reporter's forum. But regents have an ethical duty to inform the public, even if doing so may embarrass the institution or individuals. It is this type of conflict that poses an ethical dilemma for a regent.

The case presented will explore the ethical conflict a regent faces when weighing the public's right to know against the privacy rights of another regent. Variants of the case will place the administration in a position to control the student press to protect a regent from embarrassing stories and to benefit the institution. Each variant of the case will focus on the regent's potential to abuse power and the freedom of the student press.

Student Athletics

Many colleges and universities have extensive intercollegiate athletic programs as an integral part of their structure. These programs and how they are administered present unique opportunities for the review of ethical behavior. Oddly, at some schools the athletic director and/or the head coaches are hired directly by the regents rather than by the president. Furthermore, the financial affairs of the athletic programs often are not comingled with other school revenues. There seems to be an attitude of "my money" and "your money" in the area of athletics that is not carried over to other revenue-generating areas of an institution. For whatever reason, student athletic programs are often treated as separate entities and accorded special privileges beyond those granted similarly separate activities such as student housing and bookstores. This separateness of the intercollegiate athletic program in the general structure of the school does not, however, extend to the oversight responsibilities of the board of regents. Once again, the board is the final authority in all hiring, promotion, pay adjustments, and other personnel actions.

Since student athletic programs are major revenue sources for many schools, numerous opportunities for outside employment exist for successful coaches. This situation often presents issues that are difficult to resolve. Endorsement contracts with manufacturers of athletic equipment and related products are frequently handled outside of the normal procurement process because a product is not being purchased in the normal sense of the word. However, because such contracts grant the imprimatur of the institution to enhance a commercial business operation, regent involvement should be mandatory. A competitive process should be developed to generate the highest return for the school and to avoid possible charges of favoritism or conflict of interest by regents, members of the athletic department, and coaching staff.

Successful athletic programs, and even some not-so-successful ones, are often the source of financial donations to the college/university. Donors who wish to give to an athletic program are closely regulated by the National Collegiate Athletic Association. Everything from contact with potential players to job opportunities for student athletes is monitored because, if violations occur, it is the reputation of the university that is jeopardized. Maintaining the integrity of the athletic program is an important, and often difficult, responsibility of regents.

Successful athletic programs generate enormous revenue; television rights to football alone are worth many millions of dollars. Since postseason athletic contests are major sources of revenue to host cities, travel expenses and lavish entertainment are provided to virtually every member of the participating athletic programs. A regent has numerous opportunities to participate in these activities, so she or he must exercise extreme caution and careful judgment to avoid any abuse of privilege.

The case presented, and the variant on it, will focus on the ethical issues of abuse of privilege. The potential for ethical misconduct will be explored in the context of opportunities for regents to aid themselves and friends through privileges made available only to regents by an outside party. This case will also raise the issue of conflict of interest.

Campus Organizations

On virtually all college campuses, students form a variety of organizations built around a myriad of special interests. These organizations are most often created to provide an outlet for students to share like interests with other students and may range from primarily social groups, such as chess and skiing clubs, to more activist groups, such as environmental organizations. Many national and international organizations, such as the National Organization for Women and Amnesty International, are usually represented on college campuses by local student chapters, and political parties are virtually always represented through College Republicans and Young Democrats and sometimes even socialist and Marxist clubs. Many departments also sponsor clubs for students interested in particular academic subjects, and there are honorary societies for students with particularly high academic standing, for example, Phi Beta Kappa and Sigma Xi.

Students also organize through an elected student government. This government's authority is most often very limited. Indeed, the very existence of student governments is at the discretion of the administration and regents, and all authority devolves from that which is granted through official action. This is not to say that student governments may not play an important role in advising on particular issues that affect students directly. At some schools the student body president is granted a seat on the board of regents—sometimes with voting privileges, sometimes in an advisory capacity. To a significant extent, the relationship of student governments (even those having limited official authority) with the administration and regents may determine how harmoniously college and university policies are implemented.

Perhaps the most important function of student governments involves the distribution of student fees. Many fees are charged for specific activities (laboratory fees, parking fees, and mass transit passes) and therefore are discretionary on the part of the students, depending on the courses in which they enroll and their need for these specific services. Because these fees are charged for specific purposes as user charges, the revenue is transferred to the appropriate university function and is not in any way part of student government deliberations.

In contrast, another type of student fees is usually charged on a per-credit-hour basis and funds a number of general student services. These general mandatory fees, which may include libraries, student unions, and recreational facilities, are usually comingled with general university funds and allocated through administrative action. It is from this source that student governments receive the funds that they in turn may allocate to various student organizations. Sometimes these student fees are augmented with revenues from other sources that are student-related, such as profits from the student bookstore. It is a matter of administrative policy how much, if any, of general student fees or any other funds is given to student governments to allocate.

Student organizations are all creatures of the administration and regents and must be officially recognized to receive university funds. This recognition process is usually administrative and is sometimes done by the student government, but in any case recognition carries the official sanction of the regents. Student organizations receive the support of university administrations for a variety of reasons. For example, an organization may play an important general educational function for all students, faculty, and the broader community by bringing to campus well-known speakers. The work in arranging for these speakers is borne by the student organizers, thus relieving the administration of the myriad details such events require. Through these efforts, students learn important lessons in organization and cooperation in group dynamics, lessons that are difficult to teach in a classroom but can be learned through the laboratory of student organizations promoted by the administration.

A regent's role in granting official recognition to student organizations can be difficult when it becomes necessary to weigh personal beliefs with the necessity for freedom of expression. The case presented will focus on a regent who finds a particular student organization personally abhorrent. A variant of the case will address the issue of the appropriate behavior of a regent after the board has voted—but not for the position held by the regent.

How to Read the Cases

As you read the cases, you cannot help but anticipate the actions of the various parties in the case. Do not do so; instead write down your first impressions of the issues. Attempt to put yourself in the position of all parties in the case, and remember that the public is *always* an interested party to all actions of the regents. When the cases are modified to demonstrate particular points, the ethical issues involved may or may not change.

All cases are accompanied by a discussion that explores the various ethical issues. These are not meant to be answers to the problems presented but to provide a starting place for deeper discussion of the ethical questions. The discussion notes will also pose new questions as the facts of the case are amended.

In the end, a regent should be prepared to act. The purpose of holding a position of power is to use that power, and only through action can power be exercised. It is hoped that the action taken is accompanied by a thorough understanding of the ethical implications involved.

Some Guiding Principles

There are no simple rules to guide a regent so that all of his or her actions follow the highest standards of ethical behavior; however, there are some guiding principles that can be useful. These principles can best be put in the form of questions. If the answer to any of the questions is yes, then the potential for a breach of ethical conduct exists, and further consideration is strongly advised before the regent proceeds.

1. Does this action, official or unofficial, help a family member, friend, or me personally?
2. Am I getting something that I would not have received if I were not in this position of power?
3. Does this action, official or unofficial, make it difficult for the public to know what is happening at this institution of higher education?
4. Is this action, official or unofficial, an administrative issue rather than a policy issue?
5. Does this action, official or unofficial, help or hinder one particular person or firm rather than a class of people?
6. Will this action, official or unofficial, require an explanation in the press to remove any suggestion of ethical misconduct?

As you read the cases that follow, review these questions to determine the potential for ethical difficulties for regents or others in the case.

Chapter 3

Financial Conflicts

The Case of the Friendly Vendor

There really was not anything out of the ordinary in seeing Bill and Mary at the club's spring ball. They were not regulars, but then they had not been members all that long either. What was curious was the attention Bill seemed to pay to every need of Chuck and Anne. Bill would bring hors d'oeuvres, drinks when their glasses were half full, and he generally made himself indispensable.

Anne is a member of the board of regents at State University, having served as the governor's campaign chair for the county a few years ago. She was elected chair of the regents board earlier this year. Chuck, for his part, is a well-thought-of investment counselor in the trust department of the state's largest bank and everybody's odds-on favorite to succeed to the bank's presidency on the retirement of the current president.

Although Bill and Chuck had had many business dealings in the past, usually associated with Bill's architectural firm and the placement of bond sinking funds to finance his projects, his solicitous attitude, as Anne told Chuck later that night, was perhaps more related to the pending contract for a new research library at State University. She was not alarmed by this attention, however, because she had confidence that the school's well-defined bid process provided the necessary insulation from conflict-of-interest problems.

Anne had talked extensively with Chuck about the research library's financing because the arrangements were both unusual and complicated. A research library in and of itself could not provide a flow of funds to pay back the bond debt, and there had been no possibility of pledging tight general funds against the library project. The regents realized that either some other source of research-related funds would have to be found, or the project would be abandoned.

The bond underwriters had suggested that State University create a trust authority, with the school as the sole beneficiary, and funnel all research grants and contracts through the trust. The granting agencies' reimbursement to State University for overhead expenses, which would usually have accrued to the school's general fund, would be held by the trust authority and dedicated to retire the bonds. In addition, all research grants and contracts would be conducted by the trust in the name of State University, and faculty and staff conducting research would in effect become subcontractors of the trust. According to the bond underwriters, this convoluted arrangement would provide the level of assurance that bond-rating houses needed to provide an acceptable rating to finance the library.

Anne was never sure why the Research Trust was necessary when State University could reach the same goal by pledging the overhead funds and providing assurances that the general fund would be prepared to make up any shortage. She was particularly concerned that of the Research Trust's three trustees, only one was a State University regent; the other two were the SU president and the vice president for research.

Chuck's expertise was very helpful, as it had been in the past on matters of finance. Even though his bank could not be involved in any of SU's financial dealings since Anne's appointment to the board, he had given freely of his time and had even provided bank staff for educational presentations to the board on various financial subjects.

Although Anne was not a member of the new Research Trust, she was aware of the trust's affairs through the trustees' quarterly reports to the regents. She knew that the trust could award contracts without prior approval of the board and that it had significant authority independent of the SU regents. The trustees had even hired an independent in-house attorney to provide guidance on matters of contracts, personnel, and conflicts of interest. The attorney had opined that as an independent trust the trustees were not required to follow the standard SU policies on hiring, contracting, and other matters. Separate policies and procedures dealing with these issues had been set up and approved by the trustees, who had "chosen" (this was their term) to follow the state's open meeting and open records laws in most matters, although compliance was considered discretionary and was applied on a case-by-case basis.

Anne's confidence in State University's bid process was shaken two days later when Chuck related the events of a business meeting that day with Bill and the trust's attorney. He had been told that at the next trustees' meeting Bill's architectural firm, the bond underwriter, the bond counsel, and the general contractor would be announced and awarded contracts as a package on a "negotiated" basis, meaning that no bids would be solicited. Bill had set up the meeting with Chuck to add Chuck's bank to the package as the trustee bank for the bonds. Also, he had asked Chuck if he would be the fund manager of the bonds during the construction period. In all, it would be a very lucrative piece of business for the bank, somewhere in the neighborhood of half a million dollars over the life of the bond issue. The trust attorney had noted that Chuck's bank had scrupulously avoided any conflicts of interest in the past with State University because of Anne's position on the board but that in this case there was no need for concern because the Research Trust was a separate entity.

Discussion

Anne and Chuck face a dilemma. For years Chuck has been forced to pass up opportunities to bid on business with State University because of the obvious conflict of interest that Anne's position on the board of regents created. Now the legal staff for the Research Trust says that no conflict-of-interest problems exist for a particularly nice contract. Chuck is being handed a plum of a deal with no effort on his part because Anne, although a member of the board, is not a trustee of the Research Trust. Furthermore, the Research Trust has decided to let the contract without a bid process, which is the trustees' chosen way of doing business, so there will not even be the difficulties associated with a bid.

Competitive bidding processes have been established in one form or another by all public-sector entities, as well as by many private-sector firms, colleges, and universities. Competitive bidding provides two positive benefits. It can protect the integrity of the procurement process, muting charges of conflict of interest on the part of board members, and it will generally result in the lowest price being paid for the goods and/or services.

Most competitive bidding processes require that the bids be submitted by a certain date and opened publicly and read into the record. Vendors may attend the bid opening, and competitors' bids may be examined by all participants and the public at large. This process allows the vendors to act as a policing mechanism able to cry foul if favoritism is suspected.

The difficulties that arise are usually related to exceptions to the bid process. Because competitive bidding can be time-consuming, most procurement officers have the ability to make purchases valued below a stated amount without bidding. The maximum allowable purchase without a bid varies greatly from state to state, and even college to college within a state if they are independent of state general bidding laws, but the sum usually never exceeds $5,000.

Another exception is telephone bidding in the case of an emergency. This is often allowed if there is imminent threat to health, life, or property, such as the failure of an air conditioning system or in the event of a natural disaster. Telephone bidding, of course, does not provide the same protection as the open reading of written bids, but it is deemed appropriate in these emergency cases.

Sole-source contracts are another exception to competitive bidding procedures. These contracts are designed for situations in which a particular vendor sells a product that has no substitute, such as computer equipment that must be compatible with existing equipment. Replacement parts may also be deemed to require a sole-source contract when the warranty of the manufacturer has to be maintained or when no other vendor provides such parts. Sole-source contracts are for particular items and are not used to provide a contract for a particular firm unless it is incidentally the only one that carries the needed product.

Some competitive bidding processes allow the negotiation of the fees after the vendor has been selected. This is often the case with architectural and engineering contracts and other "professional services." In this process, the firm is selected on the basis of its past work and ability to complete the project, and the evaluation is made on the basis of capability rather than price.

All competitive bidding processes require that the selected firm have the lowest and *best* price. This rule allows for some discretion in the elimination of firms with either no track record in the area or past difficulties in providing services to other customers. The qualifications of the vendors to perform are examined under this criterion of selection and can result in the elimination of bids, even though they may be for a lower price. Careful documentation of why a higher bid was selected over a lower one is usually required by the bid process. All competitive bid processes have a protest period during which aggrieved vendors may challenge the outcome.

Although most college/university procurement has been exempt from general state competitive bidding laws, internal competitive bidding procedures have been put in place that follow the same general practices. It is the responsibility of the board of regents to review and approve these practices. Indeed, all purchases of the college/university are the ultimate responsibility of the board of regents, even if it does not formally take action to affirm the contracts of the procurement officers. All contracts are made with the college/university board of regents, not with a staff member or the administration.

Although competitive bidding procedures insulate regents from the decision to let a particular contract, conflicts of interest are said to exist if vendors are related to members of the board. These vendors are therefore barred from bidding. The rationale is that a possibility exists for a regent to suborn the actions of the procurement officers. A serious conflict between the public interest and the private interests of the members of the board creates a violation of ethical behavior by board members.

How close the relationship is between the member of the board and the potential vendor before a conflict is deemed to exist is usually subject to interpretation by conflict-of-interest statutes or administrative rules of some ethics commission. Higher standards may be established by the board of regents, and, if no guidelines exist outside the college/university, the board should adopt its own for members' protection.

At a minimum, a prima facie conflict exists if the relationship is first- or second-degree blood or affinity: husband, wife, father, mother, son, daughter, brother, sister, grandson or granddaughter, grandfather or grandmother, or in-laws of any of these degrees of relationship. Most statutes do not specifically define conflicts of interest that may exist in the modern world of more complicated personal relationships such as lover, "significant other," or friend, but these pose potential ethical concerns nonetheless. The true test is whether a question can be raised about an unbiased decision having been rendered in the matter.

Chuck and Anne have by all accounts conducted themselves in an ethical manner in dealing with the potential conflict of interest that would exist by SU contracting with Chuck's bank for business. This decision has worked a hardship on Chuck's employer, but the matter was presumably discussed prior to Anne's accepting an appointment to the board and was considered simply one of the costs of public service.

The Research Trust is a creature of State University, although legally the trust operates as a separate entity. It has its own board of trustees and provides only advisory reports to the SU board of regents. If we presume that this position will hold up under court scrutiny, Chuck has no legal obligation to pass up the proposed business proposition. As an ethical issue, however, the interrelationship of the activities and decisions of the SU board of regents and the Research Trust trustees presents serious problems.

One test of the potential for a conflict of interest is the degree of authority a member of the board has over the activities of the entity that is being supervised in the public interest, in this case, the Research Trust. As stated earlier, "Commerce between master and slave is despotism." The relationship between the board of regents and the administration of State University is clearly hierarchical. Power flows from the board to the administration by the authority of the board, and this power can be enhanced or withdrawn at the will of the board.

In the case of Research Trust, the central question is whether the board of regents can create an entity whose sole duty is to enhance the mission of State University but is completely independent in its actions. The elevation of the president and the vice president for research to a position of peer with a member of the board of regents presents a difficulty in determining the lines of authority. In an extreme case, the regents can mandate the activities of the

Research Trust simply by directing the actions of the president or firing the president and finding someone who will carry out their wishes. In this sense, Research Trust cannot be viewed as a separate entity because two of the three trustees do not have guaranteed independence in making decisions. The independence of the Research Trust from the regents of State University is illusory from an ethical position, even if it may be real from a legal perspective.

The alleged independence of the Research Trust in this case is not unique. Other entities maintain the same position within the constellation of college/university auxiliary enterprises. Dormitories, campus bookstores, student unions, and foundations are often placed outside the normal lines of authority of the boards of regents. Why this has been done is often a matter of historical accident, but nevertheless the arrangement places the members of the board of regents in a confused position vis-à-vis these entities.

Foundations that have as their sole mission the enhancement of the university and that use the imprimatur of the college/university in the raising of donations can, if operated independently of the university governance structure, act contrary to the policy desires of the regents. Salary supplements or expense accounts for staff and administrators, for example, may be desirable, but if not integrated into the overall policies of the regents, these perquisites may generate conflicts within the institution. Foundations are, after all, simply beneficial trusts of the college/university and as such must be accountable to the governing body that they are constituted to benefit.

Another ethical problem is posed by the activities of the Research Trust in the letting of the package contract on a negotiated basis. Regardless of whether Chuck's bank chooses to become part of the package, the contract is being let without a bid, and that poses a problem of openness in government. If Research Trust exempts itself from the open meetings and open records requirements that State University must follow, the public is denied access to information concerning the activities of a public entity. Research Trust exists for no other reason than to advance the mission of State University and is governed by three university public officials. As such, the activities of the trust must be deemed relevant to the public. A regent of State University has an ethical duty to provide open access to all school activities. The creation of a veil through the construction of a trust subverts this duty and should be a concern to all regents.

Case Variant 1

The Research Trust has determined that it will solicit bids for the package of services that will be required to finance and construct the research library. The specifications have been drawn, the bids have been received and submitted to the staff for review, and the staff will present its recommendations to the trustees. As part of the review process, one vendor has offered staff the opportunity to view his company's previous projects in other cities. The head of the review team, a member of the State University purchasing staff, has availed

himself of this offer and at the vendor's expense has
traveled to three sites, all of which seem to have been
selected for their exotic locale.

This case variant presents the problem of the role of a regent in monitoring the behavior of staff members in the bid process. Staff are required to act with the same regard for ethical behavior as regents and should have written guidelines for what actions are appropriate. Although trips to view the work of potential vendors may be considered relevant in making a thorough evaluation of a bid, bidder payment for such trips is suspect. If the evaluation process requires site visits, then it falls to State University to pay for these trips as an expense of the selection process no different from the salary of an evaluation team.

A regent who becomes aware of such action by a staff member owes a duty to the other regents to call this to their attention. Regents should in most cases nullify the bid process and request all vendors to resubmit. The offending member of the staff would presumably be disciplined and taken off the review team in the second round of bids.

All competitive bidding procedures have the option of canceling the bid process for a variety of reasons. For instance, there may not be enough bidders to give the school the best possible set of options for the purchase, the bid specifications may have been so narrowly drawn as to exclude potential bidders with a viable substitute for the product, or the market may have dramatically changed since the bid was let, as in the case of gasoline prices during the Gulf War. It is at the discretion of State University regents whether a particular request for purchase will result in a contract being let.

A "busted" bid is not without consequences, however. Vendors often expend significant resources in compiling a bid. Representatives frequently must attend pre-bid conferences, and sometimes a bid process requires that potential vendors on a short list make a presentation to a review committee or perhaps even the regents. Hours of work lie behind each submission. Schools that consistently bust bids will soon find that potential vendors will forgo the opportunity to bid, and consequently the school will draw from a narrower-than-necessary list of potential vendors. This can result in higher prices to the institution. In the face of a violation of ethical behavior, however, the board has no alternative but to cancel the bids and reopen the process.

Without written guidelines for the proper behavior of staff during bid reviews, regents become powerless to monitor ethical breaches. Guidelines should include detailed instructions about gratuities such as lunches, dinners, trips, and gifts. The training of those persons required to develop and review bids should be a continual process. This variant underscores the need for the regents to monitor the ethical conduct of staff responsible for procurement.

Summary

Colleges and universities expend significant sums purchasing goods and services each year. These purchases are an important part of the economic base of the community. In fact, in smaller communities the school may be the largest employer—not just an important part of the town's economy but the foundation of the local economic base. But regardless of the importance of the school to the local economy, the duty of regents is to the public at large, and the procurement process should be designed to provide equal opportunities to all vendors and to purchase goods or services at the lowest possible price.

This case and its variant present examples in which the public at large would not be well served if the bids were let in the manner described. Each regent has a duty to avoid conflicts of interest and *perceived* conflicts of interest, as well as monitor the ethical conduct of the staff involved in the procurement process. Ethical breaches occur on an individual basis, but it falls to each regent as a part of the group to aid in guaranteeing the ethical conduct of the board. Although some legal interpretations allow for the purchasing of goods or services from relatives of board members if the relative on the board does not vote for the purchase, this presents an ethical dilemma for those board members who must make the decision. From an ethical perspective, at a minimum, a member of the board should recuse from a vote if voting would produce a conflict of interest.

In the best of circumstances, boards are cohesive groups with a single goal: the enhancement of the educational mission of the institution they are charged with overseeing. A board member who places other board members in the position of making a decision that she or he cannot make without an ethical breach is creating another type of ethical breach. This is a subtle form of logrolling in which votes may be implicitly traded, if for no other reason than to keep peace on the board. The public cannot be properly served if each decision of the board is not arrived at with complete independence of judgment.

In the case presented, the legal issue of the independence of the Research Trust is not questioned, although it may well be. Even if there is a legal exemption from a conflict-of-interest problem, the ethical action is to decline the contract being offered. Although this course of action can, and will, cause regents and their employers to miss business opportunities, such is the cost of public service. A person who is not willing to pay this cost should not put institutions of higher education in jeopardy by serving on boards of regents.

Chapter 4

Academic Conflicts

The Case of the Helpful Regent

Regent Jones was awakened suddenly at 11:30 by the shrill ring of the telephone. This was not the first time his sleep had been disturbed during the past two months. Ever since Professor Smith had begun protesting the treatment of animals at Research Park, calls had been coming. First it was reporters wanting to know the official university position on the demands of Professor Smith. Then it was researchers who complained that their research contracts were being jeopardized by her actions. And finally it was students and parents who claimed that Professor Smith's protests were disrupting the educational process. Regent Jones, who had only six months ago been named chair of the board of regents, had almost become used to the disturbances, but this time the call caught him off guard. It was Professor Smith on the line.

A highly regarded teacher of English literature, Professor Smith was devoted to her students, and they to her. Even though her grading was rigorous and her assignments demanding, the professor's classes filled each semester. Since she was also a soft-spoken, articulate, and thoughtful woman, her almost hysterical behavior on the telephone was even more disturbing.

Regent Jones's mind flashed back over the events of the previous months. It had been a hectic and trying time ever since the new president had been approved to bolster flagging state appropriations through contract research projects from the private sector and federal agencies. The new policy had been greeted with guarded skepticism by much of the faculty as a conflict with what they viewed as the primary mission of the university—teaching. Others pointed out that research activity was also an important mission of the school and that no graduate program could be successful without graduate students' exposure to research activities.

New units had been created specifically to develop and carry out this policy, and administrative resources had been reallocated to provide writing and lobbying skills to win the coveted contracts. It was determined that the funding for overhead expenses accompanying these grants could be used to pay for teaching assist-antships. In this way, a large portion of the under grad-uate teaching assignments and much of the adminis-trative costs of the new policy would be paid. All in all, the new policy had been going rather well in Regent Jones's eyes. If success could be measured by the num-ber of dollars in contract research under way (which the president continually assured him was the proper measure), State University was in great shape.

Since the university had always had an active bio-medical research program, it was still a puzzle to Regent Jones that the contract with Medsco-Tech had raised such a furor. The work entailed implanting microchips in dogs to monitor their behavior when placed under chemical stress. Unfortunately, the tests inevitably ended when the dogs went into convulsions and died. The purpose of the contract was to map brain waves while the dogs were in drug-induced convulsions with the hope that this testing would provide new informa-tion for Medsco-Tech to develop a drug rehabilitation process for humans. The company, which ran the na-tion's largest chain of drug rehabilitation houses, was a partner with State University in one such operation on the campus of the medical school.

Regent Jones could vividly remember the first pro-test: Professor Smith had led a group of students, mostly from her literature classes, to Research Park carrying signs denouncing the treatment of the animals and the Medsco-Tech contract. Gruesome television pictures of the dogs in their last moments of life disturbed the dinner hour of the state's citizens that evening. During the next months, State University became the center of a national debate between animal rights activists and the medical research community, and Regent Jones was called on by the national media to defend the efficacy of research on living animals, the academic freedom of the medical researchers, and the Medsco-Tech contract.

He remembered the first time that Professor Smith's record as an instructor had been brought up as an issue. Her classroom lectures and assignments were attacked as nothing more than attempts to use her students as tools to advance her animal rights agenda. A group of "concerned" faculty, all of whom were in the biomedical school, had presented the president with a list of assignments that Professor Smith's students had completed during the past semester, the group's contention being that research projects investigating the use of literature in social activism were simply methods used by Professor Smith to brainwash her students. The president pointed out, however, that one of the papers on social activism presented a very thoughtful analysis of Thomas Paine's writings during the American Revolution. And, he further noted, these assignments were very similar to the ones she had been making for the past decade that had garnered praise for their creativity.

Regent Jones's head began to throb as he recalled the acrimonious meetings with the president, biomedical faculty, corporate representatives of Medsco-Tech, the chair of the English department, and the deans of the medical school and the College of Arts and Sciences. There must have been dozens of meetings with every permutation of the players. Curiously, Professor Smith had not been invited to any of the meetings and had not been chosen as a member of the Policy on Animal Research Committee, which had been hastily formed to review the existing guidelines.

Through the haze, Regents Jones began to make out what Professor Smith was saying. It seems she had gone to her office earlier that evening to grade papers and found that the door's lock had been changed. When she called the president, he had told her that her services were no longer required by the university and that she should report to the dean of arts and sciences for further clarification. Not being able to reach the dean, she had called Regent Jones.

Discussion

Regent Jones has obviously been having a rocky period as chair of the board of regents of State University. The case presents a host of administrative and ethical issues to be sorted out, and the fact that State University has been thrust into the national limelight will make a satisfactory conclusion even more difficult. Inevitably, there will be critiques and second-guessing on the part of commentators and pundits, and every action will be reviewed and re-reviewed for its "true" meaning.

Although the debate between animal rights activists and the need for animal research must be resolved by State University to the best of its ability, there is more at stake here than the contract with Medsco-Tech or even the issue of animal rights. This case pits the rights and responsibilities of faculty to pursue their research against the ethical standards of a vocal minority. In both cases— the biomedical faculty's work on the Medsco-Tech con-

tract and the class assignments made by Professor Smith—
the broader question is what limits can and should be
placed on academic freedom. That the biomedical faculty
attacked Professor Smith's academic freedom demonstrates that even they do not understand the core issue.
This adds a note of irony to the debate.

Academic freedom is both a right and a responsibility. As the term is generally used, academic freedom means
that the pursuit of knowledge shall not be abridged by administrative fiat and that no reprisals shall be made against
a faculty member because of the conclusions of her or his
research. Academic freedom is a form of freedom of
speech. Perhaps the quintessential case of the violation of
academic freedom was the excommunication by the
Catholic Church of Galileo for his work on the movement
of celestial bodies. But Mary Shelley made a powerful
and poignant case for limits to research in *Frankenstein*.
All this is to say that the academic freedom debate has
gone on for a long, long time and that the regents of State
University cannot be expected to settle the matter once
and for all.

No freedom is absolute, and this includes academic
freedom. It can be abused, and shoddy performance in
the classroom cannot be defended as an exercise of academic freedom. For instance, threats to students through
embarrassment or ridicule or attempts to force them to engage in activities that violate their personal code of beliefs are abuses of faculty power, not legitimate exercises
of academic freedom. In addition, regents and administrators have every right to monitor the classroom activity

of their faculty. This is commonly done through student teaching performance surveys and required English competency examinations for teaching assistants whose native language is not English. Also, faculty members' teaching is often evaluated by their peers through an examination of course syllabi.

In the case presented, Professor Smith invokes a higher standard to override the academic freedom of the members of the biomedical faculty to pursue their research. In her view, all of society is diminished if animals are exploited, and this loss outweighs the loss of academic freedom for Medsco-Tech's method of research. Her argument parallels that of Justice Oliver Wendell Holmes when he said that freedom of speech does not allow one to cry, "Fire!" in a crowded theater. When freedom of speech would endanger others, its abridgement is an acceptable trade-off.

The case also raises the issue of the academic freedom of Professor Smith. Regardless of the motivations of the accusers, the acceptability of Professor Smith's classroom activities has been questioned. Does academic freedom allow an individual to use the classroom as a forum to advance personal views that may or may not have any relevance to the subject being taught?

One hopes that all faculty members hold personal views on the important issues of the day—political, social, and moral. Faculty members are, after all, supposed to be thoughtful members of our society. However, an important distinction needs to be made between the in-class and out-of-class activities of the faculty. Professor Smith's ac-

53

tual protest activities (carrying signs, writing letters to the newspaper, picketing, and so on) are protected by freedom of speech as long as they do not violate unlawful assembly laws. That she is protesting the actions of her employer is not relevant. Any action by State University against her for these activities is a reprisal for a legal act and therefore unacceptable.

Professor Smith's in-class behavior is another matter. Academic freedom is not a license for a member of the faculty to subject an unwilling audience to harangues on pet peeves. State University has advertised through the college class bulletin that certain subjects will be covered in its classes. In this sense, a contract exists between the students and State University. Just how material will be presented is a matter of pedagogical choice, and discussion of topical issues is both a proper and an effective way to make a point on course material. The personal views of the faculty, if clearly stated as such, can also be an important part of students' educational experience. Just when the presentation of personal opinions crosses the line from enhancement of students' education to abuse of power is not always clear. There is a limit, however, beyond which a faculty member cannot go and expect protection in the name of academic freedom.

Regent Jones's immediate problem is what to do about the telephone call. If what Professor Smith has said is true, there will be serious repercussions from the president's summarily dismissing a member of the faculty. Even if Professor Smith had simply been reassigned or suspended, Regent Jones would be required to take official action at some future board meeting on the matter. He will probably have to judge the merit of the charges brought against Professor Smith, and any continued dialogue with her may bias his later decision. Certainly, a near-midnight telephone conversation is not the appropriate way in which to explore the matter. A polite and quick ending to the conversation is the best response, but without any promise of further action because Regent Jones cannot take sides at this point, even implicitly. The most he can promise is a fair and impartial hearing of the matter. As much as Regent Jones may wish to, he cannot be "helpful" any more than a judge can promise to be helpful to a person who is about to come before the bench. Being helpful indicates a predisposition on the case that is anathema to an unbiased decision on the issue. Regent Jones is thus ethically barred from making suggestions of possible actions or promises on the part of the board or administration, other than informing Professor Smith of her right to a hearing.

Regent Jones will have to decide whether to inform the other board members of Professor Smith's telephone call because he must also be careful not to prejudice their opinions in the matter. If the call ended quickly, then it would probably be irrelevant to the disposition of the case, and therefore no disclosure would be necessary. In any case, Regent Jones should be able to rely on Professor Smith, or her attorney, to make all salient points to the full board at the proper time.

Knowing that he will no doubt be assailed by the press the next day to explain the actions of the president with regard to Professor Smith, Regent Jones must be prepared to answer questions on a pending personnel action. This presents an ethical dilemma pitting the public's right to know against the faculty member's right to a hearing before any official action is taken by the board. Statements by any regent prior to a personnel action coming before the board as an official agenda item may be construed as indicating a predisposition on the case. Until the facts are officially presented, Regent Jones is wise to withhold any statement other than one promising to hear the matter expeditiously and open-mindedly. Unfortunately, this position will give little satisfaction to anyone.

Case Variant 1

Regent Jones has had to pay extremely close attention to the arguments of the medical school faculty and the representatives of Medsco-Tech. His attention is even greater than would be expected under these trying circumstances because for the past five years he has been a member of the board of directors of A Place for Animals, a private nonprofit group dedicated to the humane treatment of animals. Some members of A Place for Animals advocate the position that animals have the same legal rights as humans. Although this is not the official policy of the directors, the group has submitted a position paper to the board of regents of State University recommending a cessation of the Medsco-Tech contract.

Regent Jones faces a personal conflict of interest in this dilemma that pits his personal beliefs against the possible good of State University. It is not a conflict in any financial sense. He quite simply has a set of personal beliefs that must be squared with the policy debate now before the regents.

One hopes that all regents have a set of beliefs that guide their personal and professional behavior. These beliefs may be based on religious principles, moral considerations, experience, or other circumstances. Because of personal experiences, some regents may be particularly sensitive to the difficulties of students who head single-parent families or to the unique problems of students with handicaps. Another regent may strongly believe that all students should have knowledge of a foreign language to succeed after graduation. These beliefs may seem like a predisposition to a particular position on specific issues, but that is not necessarily so. Indeed, it is the duty of regents to separate their personal beliefs from public policy issues. Regents have no right to use their power to advance a personal agenda, regardless of how strongly they may feel the justice of the cause to be. For publicly supported institutions of higher education, some of these conflicts have been settled in the courts; an example is the appropriateness of public prayer.

These matters are issues of conscience and as such will have to be faced by each regent personally, with, it is hoped, tolerance of others' beliefs. The policies at public institutions of higher education must accommodate a pluralistic society, indeed encourage pluralism as a valuable part of the education process. This may mean endorsing policies for the school that would not be acceptable for the regents in their personal lives. It is left for Regent Jones to divorce himself from his private beliefs on the humane treatment of animals, although drawing from this knowledge and experience, and reach a position in the best interests of State University.

Case Variant 2

Professor Smith was able to call Regent Jones at his home at 11:30 at night on short notice because the two of them had had a romantic relationship in the past. For nearly two years prior to Jones's becoming a regent, they had developed a serious personal relationship, and although it had ended some time ago, they were still on friendly terms.

This variant presents a new set of difficulties for Regent Jones as he attempts to carry out his duties in a fair and unbiased way. The telephone call comes from someone who is more than an employee of an institution over which he has policy-making authority. The call comes from a friend in distress that he has some ability to relieve.

Regent Jones would not have been required to disclose any previous personal relationships with members of the faculty or staff prior to becoming a regent. Indeed, if he had, there would have been a host of people to list with whom he had both professional and personal friendships. This is to be expected of anyone who is appointed to the position of regent.

Regent Jones now must choose between his duty to a

friend and his duty to State University and the citizens of the state. It is probably impossible for him to render an impartial decision on the personnel action against Professor Smith; likewise, he is barred from becoming her advocate before the board or the administration. The best he can do is provide comfort to his friend as she goes through the coming ordeal and withdraw, without comment, from all actions on her case. Anything short of this would present a serious conflict of interest for Regent Jones and taint the outcome of the impending matter.

Summary

This case, and the variants on it, presents a series of difficult ethical problems for Regent Jones. Whether the issue is animal research, defense contracts, or research on human subjects, the guidelines of State University will be challenged at some time. Limits on academic freedom to pursue research are advocated by a variety of groups, and it is often in the areas of research where no guidelines exist that the greatest difficulties lie.

The political views of a faculty member can be challenged as inappropriate to a tax-supported college/university. The board of regents has a dual responsibility to promote the academic pursuit of knowledge, regardless where it leads, while ensuring that societal and intellectual standards are upheld. This case reaches no conclusion as to the appropriateness of Professor Smith's class assignments but recognizes that there are limits to academic freedom. These limits are particularly important in maintaining the proper relationship between students and faculty member. Faculty members cannot abuse their power over students and hide behind the shield of academic freedom. However, a board of regents or a president who does not defend the principle of academic freedom has abrogated his or her responsibility to the pursuit of knowledge and should not be entrusted with the management of an institution of higher education.

A variant to the case deals with the dilemma faced by a regent who has strong personal beliefs that may be in conflict with the public policy of the school he oversees. This is not an uncommon problem for a regent. It may surface in areas dealing with prayer or other religious matters, the distribution of condoms by the student health clinic, or recognition of gay/lesbian student groups. As stated earlier, it is hoped that all regents have a well-developed belief system that draws on life's experiences and other sources for guidance. This does not mean, however, that regents should not differentiate between their own personal beliefs and those that will be imposed on the university community by their public actions. Just as professors cannot use the shield of academic freedom to defend actions that are an abuse of power over their students, regents cannot use their position of power to advance their own personal belief systems.

Cases of academic freedom will always present a most difficult challenge to a regent. Perhaps solace can be found in the words of Voltaire: "I disagree with all that you have to say, but defend to the death your right to say it."

The case also points up the difficulties that will arise

if a regent has a relationship with a member of the faculty or staff. This particular case variant used the vehicle of a previous romantic relationship, but the same ethical dilemma would arise with any type of personal or professional relationship. Regents on occasion take on the role of a judge and must conduct themselves as a judge would. This means that cases cannot be discussed outside of board meetings with interested parties. In the legal system such discussions are called ex parte communications, and they are strictly prohibited to eliminate bias in regents' decisions.

Chapter 5

Personnel Conflicts

The Case of the Proud Father

Regent Harrison, of State University, could not have been prouder. As the patriarch of a family boasting seven children, he had just seen the youngest complete her MBA and pass the certified public accounting examination with the highest honors, all in the same week. It was a red-letter week for the Harrison family, which considered the education of its children as the highest priority. Regent Harrison had always felt secure that as his children took their places in the world, they would have the necessary skills and knowledge to make their own way. Each child had proved him correct.

The youngest one was following in the footsteps of her older sister Edith, a CPA at the regional office of a Big Ten accounting firm. Employed by the firm for eight years, Edith had developed into a specialist in matters of public-sector accounting and was in great demand to teach courses for the Society of Public Accounting's continuing education program.

The business college of State University, through the university's Office of Continuing Education, administered courses for the Society and provided the faculty. As a rule, the full-time faculty of the business college's accounting department taught the courses on various weekends, receiving a small additional compensation for their efforts, but Edith Harrison, as a recognized expert in the field, had been a regular member of the program's faculty for three years. It was difficult for her to take time from her other work, but the exposure to potential clients and the enjoyment she derived from teaching more than compensated for the inconvenience and a stipend significantly below her normal billing rate.

In the face of yet another budget crisis, the business college dean was facing the difficult task of trying to fill the faculty positions for required courses scheduled in the upcoming academic year. Four of the accounting department's junior faculty had left unexpectedly for the greener pastures of the private sector and other colleges. (Somehow other schools could find pay increases for incoming faculty while freezing the salaries of existing members.) Although the dean felt that staffing courses with adjuncts was not in the best interest of the student body or the professional development of other faculty members, it had become a way of life in tight budget years. After all, an adjunct cost just $2,000 per course and required no health or retirement benefits. By contrast, a full-time junior faculty member cost more than $30,000 for the same class load, plus benefits. Of course, students could see their adjunct teacher only in the classroom, and there was no requirement for adjuncts to develop new materials and publish scholarly work, but the dean saw no other solution.

He was heartened when it occurred to him that he might be able to convince Edith Harrison to teach the intermediate public accounting course, an area that had not been taught in three semesters. He knew of her work with the Office of Continuing Education and the Society of Public Accounting. In a very real way, she was ideal for the job.

The provost had given permission to the deans and department heads to make offers to prospective adjuncts without the usual screening. Typically, the adjunct appointments were forwarded to the provost, who sent them on to the president for inclusion on the regents' agenda at their meeting just prior to the beginning of the fall semester. It was not unusual, although frowned on, for adjunct positions to be affirmed formally by the regents after the adjunct had been in the classroom, sometimes for months. Since adjuncts were often paid in a lump sum at the semester's end, paperwork sometimes caught up with the appointment just prior to compensation being paid. Traditionally, there was no July regents' meeting, so it was on August 15, five days before classes were to start, that Regent Harrison saw on one of forty three agenda items the name of his daughter among some three dozen other names that were to be affirmed as adjunct appointments for the fall semester.

Discussion

This case presents Regent Harrison, the proud father, with the difficult task of determining whether the hiring of his daughter is a violation of standard antinepotism provisions. The case is complicated by a number of other features that involve ethical issues. Clearly, the father-daughter relationship is one of the closest possible relationships and would de jure fall under the antinepotism clauses in all state laws and most private-sector codes of conduct. The question concerns the degree to which an employment relationship is being entered into by Edith Harrison's appointment to an adjunct position. (Indeed, there is also the question of the relationship that has already occurred with the use of Edith Harrison by the Office of Continuing Education.) The problem Regent Harrison faces includes legal and ethical matters, as well as the process by which adjuncts are hired by the various departments of State University.

Most colleges/universities have an auxiliary enterprise center that provides space for a multitude of activities. This may be the student union or a more complete convention center, like others across the country that received start-up funding from the Kellogg Foundation. In one sense, these centers are simply fulfilling the private-sector activity of a convention site, although usually with some academic attachment to a department at the university. It is not unusual, however, for some of these activities to be undertaken simply for the profit potential. In these cases, the sponsoring organization most frequently provides speakers and pays travel and honoraria, and the school's role is simply that of a hotelkeeper.

Sometimes the school keeps financial records for the sponsoring organization and disburses payments on the organization's authorization. Although these revenues and payments go through the school's normal disbursement procedures, they cannot be construed as posing a potential ethical conflict for a regent because it is not within the authority of a regent, or the regents acting as a body, to approve or deny payments that follow this pattern.

Edith Harrison's activities for the Society of Public Accounting through the Office of Continuing Education fall somewhere in between this type of for-profit activity and a university-sponsored program. That faculty from the accounting department are used by the Society of Public Accounting does not per se make this a university-sponsored program and would not therefore create an ethical problem for Regent Harrison. The guiding principle would be the ability of a regent, or the regents acting as a board, to control the employment of a person, directly or indirectly, in the program at the university's continuing education center. The Society of Public Accounting could presumably simply move the program to a private-sector convention center or another school if it felt undue pressure was being applied in the selection of teachers.

Many colleges/universities provide continuing education that leads to certification by a regional or national organization. Again, control of the curriculum and the program instructors is the responsibility of the sponsoring organization and as such should provide no potential for conflicts of interest or nepotism problems for a regent.

University-sponsored programs that lead to a certificate or degree from the school pose an altogether different set of ethical problems. Technically, college/university degrees are awarded by the board of regents on the recommendation of the appropriate faculty group, college dean, and president. (Degrees can also be rescinded, under most unusual circumstances, only through regents' board action.) Because of this link with the degree-granting process, any and all employment by the college/university, or its auxiliary enterprise activities, falls squarely on the regents as an area of authority and control.

Edith Harrison will, with regent action, become a member of the faculty if her appointment as an adjunct is approved, and she will receive a stipend for her services, albeit less than her market wage. Regent Harrison, as proud as he may be to have a daughter on the faculty of State University, will be in direct violation of the law, as well as the ethical standards concerning nepotism. What the law provides as punishment for such a violation varies from state to state, but typically it means the forfeiture of his position of regent. As an ethical matter, Regent Harrison should resign his position, or Edith Harrison should withdraw her name, before a scandal engulfs both of them and State University.

Case Variant 1

Edith Harrison, as a senior member of a Big Ten accounting firm, was appointed to the College of Business Administration Board of Advisers. Her firm also donates funding for four undergraduate scholarships each semester and a summer internship program. The intern is chosen by a faculty committee of the Department of Accounting from applications submitted by undergraduates.

This case variant casts the dean of the College of Business Administration in the role of an accomplice to the ethical dilemma now faced by Regent Harrison. Most colleges within a university, and many departments, have advisory boards that act as a forum for the development of curricula specific to a particular discipline. These advisory boards play important roles in helping frame courses so students are better prepared once they finish their academic program. Oftentimes, advisory boards are developed to facilitate fund-raising and are coordinated by the college/university foundation and/or development office.

Although advisory boards are usually developed with the knowledge and assistance of the appropriate dean, provost, and (sometimes) the president, members are not confirmed by the board of regents, so there is no need to monitor conflicts of interest or other ethical considerations that a regent may face. Edith Harrison's appointment to the College of Business Administration Advisory Board, because it was not confirmed in any way by the board of regents, would not in and of itself raise an ethical concern for her father.

Indeed, the potential conflict of interest now exists for Edith Harrison as one who has some authority in providing her firm's funds to the business college and also as an employee of the business college. This problem needs to be resolved at her firm. Regardless of whether her father is a regent, the regents do face an ethical problem with the employment of a donor as an adjunct. It could be construed that the appointment is a quid pro quo for the donation of funds, no matter how worthy the cause. This ethical concern would not be completely resolved if Edith Harrison were to forgo any compensation because the appointment itself has value, if only honorary.

Regent Harrison has a legitimate grievance with the State University administration because of its handling of this appointment under both the general case and the case variant. It is unpardonable that he should be placed in the position that he now finds himself in. Even though the appointment of adjunct positions may not follow the same screening process as full-time faculty appointments, it is the responsibility of the administration at all levels to help regents avoid conflicts of interest. At the dean, provost, or presidential level, some query should have been made as to the possibility of a violation of antinepotism laws as a standard part of the appointment review process. It is not

the duty of the candidate to know the governing statutes
and ethical prohibitions for a particular position.

Summary

This case presents two variations of potential conflicts
with nepotism prohibitions. On the surface, prohibitions
in hiring a member of the family by an institution of
higher education are cut and dried. The pivotal question
is simply the degree of blood or affinity to the member of
the regents. This case presents more difficult problems
that arise in determining whether an employment action
has occurred. The case also raises a number of issues about
the role of the administration in helping regents avoid
conflicts of interest.

This case and its variant presume that both Regent
Harrison and Edith Harrison are persons of goodwill with
no intention of engaging in unethical or illegal behavior.
Nevertheless, the appointment of a regent's daughter to
any position within State University would be a breach of
accepted ethical behavior.

The possibility of Regent Harrison abstaining from
voting on this agenda item would in no way avoid the conflict. As a member of the board an individual regent cannot claim to have had no hand in the decisions of the
board, regardless of the individual's vote. Affirming Edith
Harrison as an adjunct would be a board decision and
therefore Regent Harrison's decision by his membership.
This position has been upheld broadly, even in cases in
which a person is employed prior to a family member's

becoming a member of the governing board. One simply cannot choose to be part of the policy-making body on some actions and not part of it on others.

Although the issue of nepotism is the focus of this case, it has broad general implications for other areas concerning personnel matters. A critical issue in all personnel matters is the determination whether the person involved is in fact an employee of the school by some definition. This case demonstrates that such a determination may not always be easily made. Nevertheless, important ethical issues are raised for a regent. All regents are bound by the same code of conduct that applies to the faculty and staff of the school, making it incumbent on a regent to demonstrate enormous caution in such matters.

Chapter 6

The Student Press

The Case of the Amateur Editor

The student press was now more than just an inconvenience. This was the last straw—a lawsuit against the City College Board of Regents by the *student* editor of the *Daily Cryer!* It was beyond Regent Cain's comprehension that an entity, ostensibly under his control, was actually engaging him in a lawsuit. The issues of the suit were straightforward: turn over documents from a regents' retreat that included his statements on the new policy for acceptable forms of expression by faculty and student body, so-called politically correct speech.

The lawsuit, of course, named the full board of regents, of which Regent Cain was but one member and not even the chair. (To Regent Archuleta fell that currently dubious distinction.) Regent Cain was understandably more upset than the other regents because of what seemed a vendetta by the *Daily Cryer* against him. From the moment of appointment, articles containing quotes from his writings and speeches had been published in an overt attempt to kill his state senate confirmation. More than one editorial had called for denial of the confirmation on the grounds that he had demonstrated insensitivity to various minority groups by using derogatory language. Regent Cain admitted that he had called more than one waitress "honey," but he would argue that it was simply a term of endearment. He viewed complaints about his other statements as equally unsubstantial.

The president of City College, embarrassed by the behavior of the *Daily Cryer,* had succeeded in restructuring the Press Advisory Board to include the regents' chair. Archuleta's attendance, when it was possible, seemed to have the desired effect, but only for short periods of time.

The creation of the Committee for the Examination of Inflammatory Speech, with Regent Cain as chair, had renewed the press's interest in Regent Cain's background. The issue of what constituted inflammatory speech was one that City College had only just begun to deal with in an organized way. With or without the interest in Regent Cain's previous statements, the board of regents would be faced with the problem of defining "hate speech" and attempting to apply penalties for violating the standards. The U.S. Supreme Court had on numerous occasions prescribed limits to freedom of speech, usually when the person was not making a political statement and was using "fighting" words to incite violence. The committee's work was going to be a difficult task in the best of environments.

A draft of the new policy, grist for the editorial page, called for the Committee for the Examination of Inflammatory Speech to become a standing committee of City College with the committee's chair serving as the chair of the *Daily Cryer*'s advisory board. It was widely believed that this draft was the work of Regent Cain in a not-so-subtle attempt to exert control over the student newspaper.

A student reporter requested a copy of the regents' retreat transcripts (at which the draft was presented) from the board secretary. At the insistence of Regent Cain, the secretary had refused the request, but in so doing, had admitted the existence of the transcripts. Regent chair Archuleta had not been informed of the request prior to the secretary's refusal.

The response of the *Daily Cryer* had been swift. A lawsuit was filed the next day demanding the transcripts and citing the state's open-records act. A front-page editorial called for the immediate resignation of Regent Cain and the repudiation of the draft version of the committee's report at the next meeting of the board of regents.

Discussion

This case presents the ethical dilemmas of two regents. Regent chair Archuleta is faced with the immediate problem of what to do with the pending lawsuit, as well as the long-term issue of how to "handle" Regent Cain. Regent Cain, for his part, faces the problem of how far he can go in his attempts to silence the student press without violating constitutional freedoms of the press and speech and the ethical standards of a regent.

The First Amendment to the U.S. Constitution guarantees freedom of religion, freedom of speech, freedom of the press, the right to peaceably assemble, and the right to petition the government for redress of grievances. The regents of City College are being challenged to wrestle with these freedoms in two different ways and for two very different purposes. Regent Cain is attempting to abridge the freedom of the press through various administrative policies to avoid what he construes as embarrassing coverage of his past. Simultaneously, the Committee for the Examination of Inflammatory Speech, a group formed for the purpose of reducing friction among various groups on campus and promoting a more harmonious educational environment, is addressing freedom of speech.

Speech codes have been adopted by a number of campuses in recent years, usually at colleges/universities that have had some outbreak of violence against a minority group. So-called politically correct speech guidelines have been extended to cover all religious groups and ethnic minorities and women. These guidelines also often include prohibitions against "gay-bashing." The rationale for such codes is that colleges/universities have a responsibility to provide an atmosphere for learning that is free from harassment and intimidation of faculty, students, and staff.

The legal foundation for these speech codes is found in various U.S. Supreme Court cases that uphold the principle that freedom of speech is not extended to words or deeds that incite violence. The Supreme Court, however, has also upheld the principle of free speech by striking down laws that prohibit free expression "simply because society finds the idea itself offensive or disagreeable," in the words of Justice William Brennan in 1989. Political speech has also been given special treatment by the Supreme Court. In cases in which speech is an attempt to express a political opinion or advance a political position, the Court has imposed virtually no limits. Furthermore, "speech," which is defined to include all actions that are an expression of an idea, is not limited to speaking or writing. A state law prohibiting the burning of the American flag was struck down as an unconstitutional abridgment of the exercise of freedom of speech.

Politically correct speech codes are attempts to limit the free expression of individuals in the name of preserving an atmosphere conducive to the educational process. No such codes have either passed or failed Supreme Court review. It is difficult to draw the line between words that incite violence and words that simply reveal the poor manners, intolerance, insensitivity, and ignorance of the speaker.

To further complicate the issue, colleges/universities have prided themselves on being bastions against intolerance of any idea, regardless of how it may offend the sensibilities of society at large or an individual in particular. This position is embodied in the concept of academic freedom. Speech codes that limit free expression at institutions of higher education must be squared against academic freedom for both students and faculty.

Regent Cain and the president of City College both seem to have transgressed in their treatment of the *Daily Cryer*. The creation of a student-press advisory board is certainly in keeping with the educational mission of the paper. Student reporters and editors are amateurs, and since the purpose of the student paper is to provide practical experience for their future careers, advice and counsel are a proper part of the educational process. However, the *intentions* of the advisory board are the ethical issue at stake, not its existence.

It is critical for the future of a free press that tomorrow's reporters' and editors' educational experiences not include the lesson that it is proper to subvert the press for the convenience of the powerful. Heavy-handed advisory boards that engage in censorship violate this principle, and a regent who engages in such activity violates proper ethical behavior. Regent Cain, with the president as an accomplice, has abused his power as a regent to protect his reputation.

Regent chair Archuleta, for his part, failed to keep the advisory board from including the regents' chair as a member and even attended a number of its meetings. Although such an advisory board structure is unusual, it is not per se either a violation of freedom of the press or the ethical code of a regent, assuming that Regent Archuleta's intentions are to provide advice rather than to have a chilling effect on the functioning of the press.

Regent Cain also abused his power as a regent when he directed the board secretary to withhold the transcripts of the regents' retreat. Since many open-records acts exclude documents that are in draft form, it is a legal issue whether such transcripts would be subject to the open-records act of a particular state. However, if the regents' retreat was an open meeting, as would be required by many states' open-meeting acts, then the substance of the meeting would be subject to the open-records act, even if there was an exclusion provided for documents in draft form. Generally speaking, regents should be prepared to provide to the press (and any other interested citizen) all documents presented at an open meeting, regardless of their status. In any case, it is prudent to err on the side of openness as a tenet of ethical responsibility to the public.

Boards of regents are more than just faceless policy-making bodies. They are groups of men and women who work together toward solutions to difficult issues. The process of wrestling with issues creates a bond and, when the process is working well, will create a spirit of camaraderie among the board members. Indeed, without a feeling of esprit de corps, the work of regents will suffer. Regent Cain's action to become personally involved in the withholding of documents of an open board meeting will test this bond among board members. Regent Archuleta faces the ethical dilemma pitting the public's right to know against the clear desire of another board member to avoid a situation that he views as embarrassing. When the lawsuit is brought to the full board for action, it will undoubtedly create a rift among the board members when each is forced to take sides.

Simply because the lawsuit involves the student press and not the "real" press does not diminish the principles at stake—the freedom of the press and the public's right to know. The issue can be resolved quickly if Regent Archuleta directs the secretary to release the documents in question. This action will preempt a divisive fight that draws in the other members of the board and a potentially protracted court battle that the college has little chance of winning. Even if the court case could be won, City College's integrity would suffer because of the message the victory would communicate to the public: that it can be excluded from some of the school's deliberations.

Case Variant 1

The *Daily Cryer* is not a publication of the journalism department of City College but an "alternative" newspaper published by a group of disaffected former student-newspaper staff members outraged by the imposition of restraints on them by the addition of Regent Archuleta to the Press Advisory Board. The reporters and editors are all students at City College. The *Daily Cryer* is distributed free on campus; stacks of the publication are placed inside the entrances to major classroom buildings and in the advertisers' stores. The publication costs are funded from personal contributions of the staff and a small amount of advertising revenue from a few local stores whose commonality seems to be their past history of run-ins with law enforcement over drug-paraphernalia-sale allegations.

The lawsuit, which not only demands release of the transcripts of the regents' retreat but also requests a restraining order against the City College police, alleges that the campus police have been systematically picking up copies of the publication and destroying them. It further alleges that the police have harassed individuals who have attempted to hand out the *Daily Cryer* to students as they enter and exit classes.

Although the facts of this case variant differ with respect to the school's role in the *Daily Cryer,* the ethical issues of freedom of the press and the public's right to know remain the same. The freedom of the press issue is expanded, however, to include not only the release of the regents' retreat transcripts but also the question of the free distribution of a nonschool publication on campus. That the *Daily Cryer* is a nonschool publication ironically makes it a more "real" publication in terms of the administrative oversight of the board of regents. That the reporters and editors are all students and that the publication will in all probability have a short life are irrelevant. The *Daily Cryer* has the same legal status as the state's morning newspaper.

The ethical tenet that the public has a right to know

the activities of its public institutions is still the question in this case variant. The entity that has requested documents is changed, but the principle on which this request is based has not. Regent Archuleta will probably receive more criticism from other board members if he unilaterally directs the secretary of the board to release the transcripts, but the ethical foundation of such an action is just as sound.

Another issue is raised that goes to the heart of freedom of the press. Various court cases have established the principle that attempts to limit the distribution of publications are a constitutional violation of freedom of the press. City ordinances that limit the location and number of news distribution boxes have been struck down by the courts on this basis. No distinction has been made between free publications and those that require purchase. Government harassment of "pamphleteers," the term used at the time of the American Revolution, was one of the reasons that this principle was established in the First Amendment of the Bill of Rights. The use of police power to limit the distribution of ideas is anathema to Americans and is well protected by the courts. This variant, rather than diminishing the ethical issues by reducing the credibility of the *Daily Cryer,* actually increases the stakes dramatically.

Regent Archuleta's position is certainly no less enviable. To settle the lawsuit, the board will be forced to affirm the principle that the campus police are not to harass those persons who wish to distribute their publications on campus. This will require a public repudiation of past actions and will seem like a personal insult to Regent Cain.

The affirmation of the principle of freedom of the press is not the same as agreement with the editorial position taken by the *Daily Cryer* with respect to Regent Cain, although this not-so-subtle point will no doubt be lost on Regent Cain.

Case Variant 2

Regent Cain has decided that he has felt the sting of the *Daily Cryer* for the last time. Even though it is the student paper of the institution on whose governing board he serves, he files a libel suit against City College, the student editor, and the faculty adviser, both in their official capacity with the paper and as individuals. He asks for a monetary award for the damages done to his reputation by the editorials.

This case variant presents an extreme response by a regent to the criticism that comes naturally to anyone in a position of authority in a public body. Regent Archuleta's role as chair is now, made easier by Cain's suit. Since he cannot sue himself, Regent Cain must resign his position on the board if he is to pursue the suit against City College. Furthermore, any suit against the student editor or the faculty adviser, even in their private capacity, would by necessity include City College because the alleged libel was published in the school paper.

Student newspapers can and are sued for libel; however, for a regent (now a former regent) to sue would be most unusual. Nevertheless, this variant points to an important difference between a private-sector paper and a student paper of a public institution of higher education. In this case, public, rather than private, funds are at stake in any legal settlement. Furthermore, most states have sovereign immunity statutes that limit the liability of the state or its agencies. This variant also points out that total lack of control of the student press can lead to potentially disastrous financial consequences for the school.

The acceptable point of control of the student press, however, is not in censorship or prepublication review of the material to be published but in the selection of the people who will put out the paper. A careful review of the journalistic skills and maturity of those who will be given the burden of the student press is a proper safeguard for the institution. Actions beyond this would approach manipulation of the press.

The legal issues of the suit brought by former Regent Cain are beyond the scope of a discussion of the ethical questions presented by this case variant. However, members of a board of regents of a public institution are probably considered "public figures" in the eyes of the law, meaning that all aspects of board members' lives and behavior are subject to review and comment in the press. Without the finding of malice, which is particularly difficult to prove in cases involving a public figure, there is little likelihood that Cain will successfully win his libel suit. The remaining board members must remember, however, that their duty is to City College, regardless of any personal relationship developed with Cain, and any communication with him on the subject of the case would be a conflict of interest. The fallout from Cain's lawsuit will certainly continue for a long time.

Summary

This case and its variants raise a number of issues regarding freedom of the student press as part of the general principle of freedom of speech. Americans hold these freedoms sacred as indicated by their status in the Bill of Rights, and as such they form the foundation on which the ethical principles of a regent may be based. That the student press is the product of a college-funded student laboratory within the educational process does not diminish the paper's status as a vehicle for the public's right to know the activities of its public institutions of higher education.

The student press, with varying degrees of success, is part of the public's access to the news. It is the duty of the school and the board of regents to make this newspaper an excellent educational experience for students as they prepare to enter the private-sector press corps. If they are taught poorly, they will serve the public poorly. Perhaps the worst lesson they can learn is that it is proper for the press to avoid a story that finds disfavor with a person in power. The duty of all members of the press is to all readers, not just a select few. This is the principle on which the press is accorded such protection under the Constitution.

The case also demonstrates that freedom-of-speech issues are not so simple. The Committee for the Examination of Inflammatory Speech is charged with designing a code specifically for the abridgement of free expression, presumably with penalties for violators. The very attempt at such a code assumes that there are proper limits to free speech. The courts have severely limited such abridgements but do recognize that incitement to violence is one. What can be termed *incitement* in a case in which no violence took place is difficult to say. And it is exactly this type of situation that is the target of such codes. For institutions of higher education, where academic freedom and unfettered pursuit of inquiry are prized, codes that monitor free expression raise particularly difficult questions.

The ethical issues faced by a regent in the areas of freedom of the press and freedom of speech can pit the power of a regent to manipulate the press to his or her own ends against the perceived good of the college to put forward a positive image of itself. Private-sector firms have the latitude to deal with internal dissent in a private way. Public-sector institutions, by the very fact that they are public, are most often forced to air any stresses or differences publicly. Manipulation of the press by a regent is an abuse of power and a breach of ethical behavior, even if the intent is to preserve the reputation of the institution and not the reputation of an individual member of the student body, faculty, staff, or regents.

Chapter 7

Student Athletics

The Case of the Ardent Booster

Regent Jackson was a *fan*. About this no one had any doubt. He became a fan only after leaving the hardwood (some twenty-five years ago), where he had distinguished himself by winning All-American honors three years in a row and a national championship for State University. This is not to say that Regent Jackson was not concerned about the other activities of State University. It had been his SU education, after all, that had afforded him a comfortable living. But although he appreciated and valued his educational experiences, everyone knew that Regent Jackson was a die-hard fan of his alma mater's athletic teams.

The State University basketball team, which had been through both good times and bad since Regent Jackson was a star, was currently enjoying one of the good times. A national championship seemed within grasp. The play-offs had gone well, and the players and coaches were confident—but not cocky, as they say.

These events were always exciting. Alumni who had not given a thought to their school in years were overflowing with school spirit and clambering for a victory—and tickets. The State University Foundation, which always purchased a large block of tickets for just such occasions, was dispensing them with the care one would expect from an organization whose success was measured in only one way: dollars donated. Of course, the athletic department was buried in requests far beyond its ability to comply. The national championship was, after all, going to be decided in beautiful and exotic Hawaii.

Honolulu had competed with nearly a dozen other sites for the privilege of sponsoring the national championship. City officials had gone all out with promises of lavish banquets for the dignitaries of the two competing schools, golf tournaments at the most exclusive courses, harbor tours, and of course, appropriate athletic facilities for the event. Although the budget was enormous, the Convention and Tourism Center directors felt the money was necessary to promote tourism. Besides, the whole cost (and more) would be covered by the hotel/motel tax and the fees charged for television coverage.

The National Championship Sponsorship Committee sent the SU athletic department its allocation of the number of people who would be covered by the special events, including how many would be entitled to free hotel rooms, meals, golf green fees, and so on. Dutifully, the athletic department forwarded the allocation to the president of State University after subtracting what was considered the appropriate number for use by coaches, staff, spouses, and members of the All Sports Club, a fee-paying organization of former athletic greats loosely sponsored by the athletic department. The university president then forwarded the allocation to the foundation for its use after, of course, subtracting what she considered the appropriate number for senior school staff, deans, and other dignitaries, including members of the board of regents. The budget was, as stated, enormous.

Now it had been the tradition for the national champions of 1970, Regent Jackson's team, to gather at sporting events for camaraderie and barbecue. Since the athletic department and alumni office encouraged such gatherings, the foundation tried to accommodate requests from such groups. Members of championship teams, who were also members of the All Sports Club, were virtually assured of tickets.

Regent Jackson's secretary entered his office as white as a sheet. It seemed that the man on the telephone was in such a state of distress that he was incoherent, blubbering that he had to "see the game or die." Regent Jackson took the call with apprehension, only to find that one of his long-lost teammates had been told by the foundation office staff that all tickets had already been allocated and that, regardless of his status as a former champion, he would have to go to a ticket broker in Honolulu if he wanted to see the game. He was not a member of the All Sports Club, of course.

Discussion

Regent Jackson's dilemma illustrates the problem of how to determine the ethical limits of a regent's power. Although presented in the context of an athletic contest, the problem can easily surface in any number of situations. These include the admission of a substandard student to a course of study (an academic matter) or the assignment of students to particular campus dormitories, some dorms being preferred over others (an administrative affair). Any department of a college/university that includes an allocation mechanism amendable by staff action is potentially subject to abuse of power by a regent.

Abuse of power also covers a regent's acceptance of privileges not related to the duties of a regent and not afforded members of the public. In the modern world of big-money athletics, where sporting events are staged for the benefit of local economies, perquisites are frequently proffered. In the private sector the offering of such "perks" is standard practice by hotels, convention centers, and resorts in their attempts to gain corporate business. For a person in a position of public trust, these "freebies" can present an ethical problem and perhaps raise a legal question.

A regent's duties include oversight and policy-making for all activities of the school, including all extracurricular activities, such as intercollegiate athletic events. Attendance at these events can be rightly construed as part of the duties and responsibilities of a regent, and tickets provided by the school (but paid for by the regent at market prices) would not normally constitute an abuse of power. However, special seating and other arrangements that are not provided to other ticket holders and are not part of the regent's official duties present potential ethical problems.

Major sporting events, and other regional or national extracurricular competitions, present added problems. Here the event is away from the school, and arrangements for meals and lodging are often part of the event's "package." Additional ethical difficulties exist when special activities such as golf tournaments and banquets accompany the sporting event. Some activities can be considered part of the regent's official schedule whereas others are so thinly disguised that one needs caution to differentiate them. One test is whether the regent would feel comfortable submitting a request for payment from school funds for the true, full cost of the activity. However, sometimes it is *access* that is the privilege and that presents the ethical dilemma. Use of exclusive golf courses (the operative word being "exclusive") is just such a case.

Regent Jackson is presented with the difficult task of aiding a former friend and teammate by an exercise of his power as a regent. Clearly, he is being asked to call the athletic department and/or foundation and have his friend's name substituted for another person's name on the ticket list. If he does so, Regent Jackson will be subverting the university's system of allocation.

Most collegiate systems are loosely structured for just such events, but this does not eliminate the ethical problem of abuse of power. Athletic department staff will feel pressure to respond to even the most casual telephone call from a regent concerning the plight of a friend. The request need not even be explicitly articulated by Regent Jackson for the person fielding the call to feel his exercise of power. The same is true for calls to the foundation. Even though a separate entity, the foundation's mission is the development of State University, thus placing it in the same ethical territory as any other SU department.

Case Variant 2

The budget crisis affecting all academic departments had not spared the State University athletic department. Even coaching staff salaries had been frozen in the last budget crunch. When Coach Velásquez was approached by the Swish Shoe Company sales representative with an offer for free athletic shoes for all team members plus a handsome fee for speaking at the sales-staff retreat on his "research" findings after using the shoes, it was a gift from heaven! Besides, Swish was certainly a competitive shoe, and the company's offer would save the athletic department budget nearly $100,000 per year, or two assistant coaches' salaries. Coach Velásquez simply had to sign the requisition for Swish Shoe as a sole source.

This case variant presents an ethical dilemma for Coach Velásquez, and if he forwards the offer through channels, the board of regents will have to face the ethical problem of using the imprimatur of State University for commercial purposes. An examination of the university's chain of command is pertinent in this case variant. An academic department is headed by a chairperson who typically is chosen by the department's faculty and officially appointed by the dean of the college in which the department's budget is located. The dean of each college (Arts and Sciences, Business Administration, and so on) reports to a provost or, in the absence of a provost, the president, who is directly responsible to the board of regents. These titles may vary. Perhaps the senior university officer is called a chancellor and the senior academic officer is titled president rather than provost. There is, however, a clear hierarchical structure from the faculty through a senior academic officer.

Curiously, even though most athletic departments are also part of the academic structure of the school, people who are part of the coaching staff often hold hybrid positions that are partly academic and partly staff. Moreover, it is not unusual for the athletic director and head coaches to be hired directly by the board of regents in a manner similar to the president's selection. In fact, at some schools the athletic director reports directly to the regents rather than to the president. No other officer in the academic hierarchy is given such status. This organization of the athletic department puts greater responsibility on regents and can potentially place the president in conflict with the athletic director in a regents' meeting.

The development of this unusual organizational structure has been decades in the making and would take an equal number of years to change. This structure is partially responsible for much of the grief that comes to regents from athletic programs because regents are direct supervisors of an area of the school and unable to delegate this responsibility to the president. Adding to the problem is the fact that regents have neither the time nor the staff to supervise properly the day-to-day activities of a specific school function, especially one that can be as enormous as a college/university athletic program.

In this case variant, Coach Velásquez should have in his possession a written regents' policy that anticipates such offers as the one made by Swish Shoe. The specific chain of command when such an offer is presented should be stated clearly in the policy, making it easy for Coach Velásquez to do the right thing. State University is selling a commodity, a sale that should be handled through the normal bid procurement process. Crass as this may seem, State University simply sells the exclusive use of its team's feet to the highest bidder. This method guarantees that no side payments are being received and that State University gets the greatest revenue for its "services."

Such offers are not limited to the athletic department. Selection of textbooks provides some of the same possibilities, as does the use of special equipment in laboratories and by the school band or orchestra. These offers become an ethical issue when a quid pro quo exists for use of the school's reputation to enhance a commercial enterprise's bottom line.

Summary

This case presents a host of ethical issues dealing with the conduct of the State University athletic department. Even though the organizational structure of the athletic department is typically different from that of other extracurricular-activity departments (theater, orchestra, band), they all can be faced with the same ethical dilemmas.

Foremost is the issue of perquisites provided to regents. When outside entities, such as the National Championship Sponsorship Committee, provide these benefits, they may be more substantial in nature, but the ethical issues are the same, regardless of the intrinsic value of the perk. The test that must be passed is whether the activity is part of the official business of the institution. Acceptance of benefits that do not pass this test is an abuse of power. Simply paying for the ticket may not bypass the abuse-of-power problem because a person's place on a list has value, often exceeding the out-of-pocket cost of the ticket. (In a particularly acrimonious divorce, the season football tickets of a perpetually highly ranked university were hotly contested. It was *access* to these tickets that was at stake, not the tickets per se.)

The case also presents another potential abuse-of-power ethical problem in the booster's request for special treatment by the school in allocating its tickets. Yielding to the temptation for a regent to call a member of the staff to make an "inquiry" may in and of itself not be an abuse of power; however, in some sense there is no such thing as a "simple inquiry" by a regent because of the level-of-

95

power differential between the calling regent and the answering staff person. It is difficult for a staff person to not accommodate a person in power making a request, even if it is unstated. All such calls by a regent of an inquiry nature, if such calls are made at all, should be to the next person in the chain of command, the president or a vice president. This minimizes the difference between the levels of power. Quite simply, a president will have an easier time saying no than a clerk deep in the organization. A regent has *less* power to "work the system" than an average citizen because of the regent's position of trust.

This case also presents the ethical problem of a private enterprise using the school's name as an advertising vehicle. Whether State University wishes to pursue these potentially revenue-generating activities is a matter for the regents to determine in a discussion of the issue. The school's reputation is a valuable commodity. Consequently, the use of the school in any form as an advertising vehicle should be considered by the regents as a procurement situation. That is, the school's reputation and imprimatur are owned by the institution, not by members of the staff, including coaches.

Abuse of power is a delicate ethical issue and is often found in the eye of the beholder. Regarding a member of a public body with responsibilities to the public at large, the beholders will be citizens who may have no chance in their lifetimes of traveling to Hawaii for a luxurious vacation. Regents should be mindful that the public *perception* of their behavior may be as important as any rigid guidelines in determining what constitutes abuse of power. This important concept was perhaps said best by Marcus Cornelius Fronto two thousand years ago in a letter to Marcus Aurelius: "It is true that he who ignores the reputation of virtue ignores, also, virtue itself."

Chapter 8

Campus Organizations

The Case of the Outraged Regent

In some ways it was a tempest in a teapot, but it had polarized the campus as nothing had since the Vietnam War protests. Groups were springing up like mushrooms after a warm rain, each with its own indecipherable acronym and ardent leader. An unofficial count put it at six groups against and eight groups for. There was no coordination among the various factions, and there was sometimes open hostility among those on the same side of the issue. "We have our own reasons" seemed to be the only point on which they could all agree. On one level, the battle was over $1,200 in student activity fees.

Each year the Ways and Means Committee of the student government of State University allocated student fees granted to it by the administration for the various officially recognized student organizations on campus. In most years some groups received no funds at all, the argument being that it was best for the student body to have a few organizations that had enough funds to do a significant job rather than many organizations with virtually no funds. This policy was implemented at the discretion of the Ways and Means Committee, but required affirmation by the entire student government membership. Within even the short institutional memory of the student government, however, precedent could be cited for granting some funds to all requests in the name of democracy. This did not seem to be one of those years.

The Gay/Lesbian Educational Effort (GLEE) had secured a faculty sponsor and duly applied for funds to promulgate the goals of its organization. The GLEE application had been received by the Ways and Means Committee and reviewed for its educational content and breadth of appeal to the student body, the two most critical criteria stated by the committee when it had issued the call for proposals. But it now seemed that there would be no funds granted to GLEE, regardless of the merits of the proposal, because the Ways and Means Committee had rejected the organization's application, deciding that GLEE was not to be considered an official university student organization. In this status as an unrecognized organization, GLEE was ineligible for student activity funds ipso facto. The merits of the proposal were thus irrelevant. The controversial organization vowed to override the vote of the Ways and Means Committee in the student government body as a whole, and thus began the debate.

The issue had been raised to the national level, with groups having more well-known acronyms joining those hastily created by the students and some of the faculty. Regent Kim had been watching the developments with chagrin. That a committee of the student government could embroil the school in what Regent Kim considered a national disgrace was beyond his level of tolerance. He was as pleased with the Ways and Means Committee's stand as he was distressed that such an organization as GLEE might both receive official university recognition and the use of the public's money to promulgate what he considered disgusting and immoral behavior. He bolstered his case against recognition of GLEE with the state statute declaring homosexual acts unlawful.

When he thought he had received all the surprises that this issue could bring, he was shocked when Regent Robyns called and said she was going to ask to speak during the student government debate and wanted Regent Kim's aid in convincing students to grant recognition to GLEE. Regent Robyns hoped to get as many regents as possible to come to the meeting and show support for recognition. She argued it would be best if the issue was settled by the student body because it was the right thing to do, and in any case the American Civil Liberties Union would sue the university to force recognition. Since Regent Robyns was on the board of directors of the state chapter of the ACLU, she knew whereof she spoke.

Discussion

The case presents two different regents with very different views on the student government recognition of GLEE. Each in his or her own way faces an ethical dilemma. Regent Kim must determine how his personal abhorrence of homosexuality can be reconciled with the desire of part of the student body to form an organization in support of gay life styles. (With a grimace, he had read GLEE's motto: "Gay and Proud.") Regent Robyns, with a more tolerant attitude toward homosexuality, faces a conflict of interest in her position as a board member of an organization that may well sue the institution she is charged with governing. In a very real way Regent Robyns could be viewed as suing herself.

From a regent's perspective, the root of this case is official university recognition of a student organization. With such recognition come certain privileges, one of which is potential access to funds from student fees. Also, student organizations are typically granted access to school facilities for meetings, free space in the student newspaper to announce meetings, and tax-exempt status if someone chooses to donate funds to the organization. The financial records of student organizations are usually maintained by the university in university bank accounts at a cost to the school.

The process by which universities grant student organizations official status varies, but at State University the authority to confer official recognition to student organizations had been delegated to the student government, at least as far as the allocation of student activity fees was concerned. Ultimately, of course, regents are the only ones who can grant the special privileges conferred by official recognition of a student organization. This follows from the fact that the student government, as independent as it may seem, exists only on the authority of the regents. Furthermore, all funds that the student government allocates come from the treasury of the school and therefore must be distributed by regent action. In short, all regents are a party to the actions of the student government, and they cannot avoid responsibility for these actions by arguing that the student government is an independent body.

Regent Robyns' plan to lobby the students in their deliberations, however, raises a significant ethical problem. Regardless of her motives or the conflict she faces as a board member of the ACLU, regental involvement in the deliberation process of a duly constituted body of the university is an abuse of power. There is no difference between lobbying the student government and lobbying a faculty committee deliberating the tenure of a member of the faculty. Regents will ultimately have their say on the matter, but involvement at a level prior to a regents' meeting is tantamount to suborning the process and is a flagrant abuse of power, regardless of the best motives and intentions. If groups to which regents have delegated authority are deemed to use it irresponsibly, regents have every right, and indeed the responsibility, to withdraw that authority; but until that is done, any involvement not part of the deliberative process is a serious breach of ethics.

Regent Robyns also has a significant conflict-of-interest problem as a member of the state board of the ACLU. That the ACLU is not a business enterprise having dealings with State University is irrelevant; conflicts of interest do not always have to be financial in nature. Not-for-profit organizations that make requests of the university for use of facilities and other privileges, not an uncommon occurrence, can present a serious conflict-of-interest problem for regents. As a person representing a not-for-profit organization through board membership, a regent, as a member of the university governing board, cannot simply ask the university for special consideration. This is nothing more than asking oneself for special privileges that are financed by taxpayers.

That Regent Robyns is only one member of each board does not in any way reduce her conflict. The device of recusing from a decision, that is, withdrawing on a particular agenda item, does not eliminate the conflict. All actions of a board are the actions of each individual, regardless of how a particular regent voted. Furthermore, that other board members know that one of their members has a personal interest in the outcome of an action can lead to logrolling. Simply put, the existence of a personal interest by a board member makes it more difficult for the other members of the board to make an impartial decision, which is the essence of the deliberative process. In a very real way, it is inappropriate to place other members of the board in the awkward position of deciding an issue while another board member looks on with a personal interest at stake. Regent Robyns must choose which of her duties is primary and resolve her conflict by resigning from one of the two boards.

Regent Kim faces a more complex ethical dilemma. His personal beliefs are clearly at odds with those of the members of GLEE and presumably with those of many of the others in the university community who have organized in support of recognition. He must divorce his personal beliefs from his public responsibilities and make an appropriate decision for the governance of the school, although this action requires a level of tolerance that he may not, and indeed need not, have in private life.

In June 1995 the U.S. Supreme Court ruled in *Rosenberger* v. *University of Virginia* that a Christian student publication must be granted student fees on the same basis as all other student organizations. The majority held that to do otherwise is an abridgement of freedom of speech and would exclude the work of "hypothetical student contributors named Plato, Spinoza and Descartes." GLEE has the same protection of freedom of speech as the University of Virginia Christian magazine. Regent Kim's dilemma is the conflict between his personal values concerning homosexuality and the values embodied in the U.S. Constitution.

Often it is not clear when a regent's personal beliefs must become subservient to the higher authority of the Constitution. Many cases arise in which guidance is found in the simple maxim that tolerance is a virtue. Remembering that universities are places designed to foster ideas (many of which will be discarded with time) can help a regent avoid the ethical breach of using his or her position to promulgate a belief system.

Case Variant 1

During enrollment in the semester following the official recognition of GLEE by the university, forty students refused to pay their full tuition and fees. They withheld the portion of their fees that they calculated were used to fund GLEE, some $1.25. Not being satisfied with this personal statement, they staged a rally in front of the administration building and urged other students to do the same. Regent Kim addressed the rally and announced that he would introduce a motion to the board to allow a fee "checkoff" for students wishing to designate the use of their fees.

These forty students have availed themselves of the right to peaceably assemble to seek redress of their grievances. To the extent that such a demonstration remains peaceful and within the legal bounds set for the time and place of demonstrations, any action to disburse the students violates their rights. The demonstration in and of itself presents no ethical dilemma for any of the regents. Regent Kim, however, has chosen to aid the demonstrators in their cause against the university. This action is a serious breach of ethics.

Regents, when granted power to make policy decisions for the conduct of the affairs of their school, are given a unique position to argue, make motions, and present views to the other regents in a way that no other person can. Also, a regent is given the power to cast a vote that will help determine the ultimate outcome of the issue. Once decided, however, a regent is ethically bound by the decision of the board; the actions of the board are the actions of each member individually. Ethically, Regent Kim must confine his use of power to the venue of the board meeting and forgo the use of rallies, newspaper editorials, and other avenues to make a case for board action that he favors.

Another conflict of interest is revealed in this case variant. Regent Kim is presumably in favor of the students' act of civil disobedience in withholding a portion of their student fees. Regardless of the reason, students who do not pay their full tuition and fees are barred from class attendance and dropped from the rolls. This is regent policy that Regent Kim is bound to uphold and indeed obligated to seek assurance that the administration is following. By encouraging students to engage in this act of withholding fees, Regent Kim is encouraging the breaking of a university policy that he helped set. This presents a conflict of interest between his duty to the university and his views concerning the use of student activity fees. As with Regent Robyns, Regent Kim must choose which duty he feels is paramount and either not speak at the rally or resign from the board and attempt to influence the regents' decisions from the outside as an interested citizen. In the capacity of an outsider, of course, he would not have the privilege of introducing a motion for a policy of a student fee checkoff.

Summary

Colleges and universities occupy a unique place among the social institutions in America. Free and open discourse is not only encouraged and protected but also rewarded. Academic freedom is designed to maintain this openness by protecting ideas that may be viewed by some as contrary, distasteful, or even immoral or dangerous. Academic freedom is simply the term for the freedom of speech granted and protected by the First Amendment of the Constitution. Students and their student organizations are accorded this same protection, even if that protection goes against the doctrine of separation of church and state (*Rosenberger* v. *University of Virginia*).

Regents have an obligation to guard this freedom of expression, even in the face of conflict with their personal codes of morals and conduct. Allowing others to express their views is not the same as condoning those views. This case implies that some of the organizations supporting the recognition of GLEE are doing so based on this principle rather than because homosexuality is acceptable to them personally.

The conflict between Regent Kim's personal beliefs and those held by a university student organization pits freedom of expression by students against a regent's view of appropriate behavior—a view that is probably held by a significant number of the taxpayers in his state. It is the importance of protecting the views of a minority group that gave rise to the First Amendment of the Constitution. As long as any student organization is accorded privileges, such as funding from student activity fees, all student organizations must be guaranteed the ability to compete for these privileges on an equal basis.

This case also points to the limits a regent has in trying to influence the outcome of the deliberative process of a properly constituted policy advisory group within the university. Regent Kim's attempt to influence the student government was a serious breach of ethics because it constituted an abuse of power. A regent will ultimately have an opportunity to decide on the policy of the school at a board meeting, and it is only there that a regent's views may be properly aired. The case presented this problem in the context of a student government decision, but it could just as easily have been the promotion and/or tenure of a controversial member of the faculty, the retention and/or admission of a low-performing student, or something as benign as the granting of honorary degrees. Each situation is subject to a process created by the regents and subject to their final approval. If the regents do not wish to delegate to committees the authority to provide advice on policy, it is their prerogative to abolish them. Attempts to suborn them, however, are an abuse of power and a serious breach of ethics.

The case also presented two different conflicts of interests: Regent Robyns with her position on the board of the American Civil Liberties Union and Regent Kim in his behavior as a supporter of the student rally to withhold a portion of assessed fees. A conflict of interest can and does exist if an individual holds a position with an organization that is attempting to influence the policies of the university governing board on which that same person sits as a regent, regardless of whether the organization is not for profit or for profit. It is not necessary for financial gain to be at stake for a conflict of interest to exist. Any interests that compete with those of the university are conflicts of interest for a regent because they cloud her or his ability to make impartial decisions in the *exclusive* best interest of the school.

The conflict of interest Regent Kim faced when deciding to speak at a rally designed to influence university policy raises a further issue, one that all regents face at one time or another (unless they always vote with the majority on all issues). The actions of the board are the actions of *all* members of the board, regardless of how an individual regent voted on the issue. The use of outside influence to change a policy of the board after a vote, whether it be by letters to the editors of newspapers, appeals to the state legislature for statutory changes, or speeches to Rotary Clubs, is divisive and unethical. Regents must remember their ability to influence policy with their votes. If a regent feels so strongly on a particular issue that he or she cannot support the board's decision, the only ethical action is to resign.

Summing Up

These cases have presented a variety of different situa-tions that place regents at ethical crossroads. Although the cases are developed around particular factual situations, each can be generalized to broader issues, and from a legal perspective each case (or ethical dilemma) has an answer. But ethical issues cannot be settled simply on the basis of a legal solution. The law provides no guidance to a regent who has strong personal feelings, for example, concerning an issue before the board that conflicts with her or his religious beliefs. This situation pits the regent's personal belief system against the requirements that all regents' actions be in the interest of the public at large, a public that may not share the same value system. Regents are always balancing this requirement to serve a multi-cultural, pluralistic society and a personal value system. It requires tolerance of other belief systems to retain this sense of balance.

Earlier in this book a set of suggested guiding prin-ciples was offered in the form of questions that a regent may ask to indicate the possibility of an ethical breach. In summary, perhaps these questions can be reduced to a simple dictum: put the interests of the public above all other interests—even though following this dictum may cause hardships in the form of lost income, lost privileges, and lost friends.

There is little solace in being an ethical regent. It seems that the world conspires to place ethical problems in your way. As with all such matters, acting ethically becomes easier once you affirm that ethical considerations will always be part of your decision-making process. Fewer problems will then be placed in your path. The personal, satisfying feeling that comes from "doing the right thing" will be the ultimate reward. Expect no other.